ORTHOCRACY SPEAKS

a layman's guide to the ruling system

by George Trinkaus

**High Voltage Press
Portland**

On first looking into Orthocracy Speaks, a great orthocrat (in a rare breach of Rule 12) shows his weariness. Photo found on Drudge. Orthocracy speaks on Obama and his office on page 95.

to James Boswell

copyright © 2013
by George B. Trinkaus
All rights reserved.

Designed at Eberhardt Press

ISBN 978-0-9709618-9-1

to Stephen

ORTHOCRACY
SPEAKS
a layman's guide to the ruling system

by George Trinkaus

High Voltage Press
Portland

Contents

Preface 1

Part One.
Roll over, Machiavelli 9

Part Two.
Orthocracy Parses the 13 Rules of Rule 29
1. *Keep them weak.* 29
2. *Keep them dumb.* 33
3. *Keep them scared.* 35
4. *Control all resources.* 37
5. *Divide and conquer.* 39
6. *Control their rhythm and pace.* 41
7. *Control their chemistry.* 43
8. *Control their sex.* 45
9. *Jack them around.* 48
10. *Use coercion routinely, brute force when necessary.* 49
11. *Use deception routinely, the Big Lie when necessary.* 51
12. *None of this can show.* 54
13. *This is The System; there shall be no other.* 56

Part Three.
Orthocracy Speaks on the Issues of the Day 61
1. *Afghanistan* 68
2. *Guantanamo* 72
3. *Solitary Confinement* 73
4. *Iraq.* 76
5. *The Economic Collapse* 80
6. *Privacy* 82
7. *Energy* 84
8. *Mountain-top Removal.* 90
9. *The Gulf Oil Spill.* 92
10. *Barrack Hussein Obama.* 95
11. *Immigration* 98
12. *Chemtrails, Black Helicopters, UFO's, Men in Black* .. 100
13. *Drone Attacks.* 102

Preface

ARE WE GOVERNED BY A PHILOSOPHY OF RULE that goes unperceived and unspoken? Is there a hidden technology of rule? I say, yes. Moreover, I contend that the real rules of rule are unutterable and that one of those rules itself (Rule 12) dictates that they be forever unutterable. Rule 12 says, "None of this can show."

Woodrow Wilson wrote in 1913 that powerful men know that there is another power somewhere "so organized, so subtle, so watchful, so interlocked, so complete, so pervasive, that they had better not speak above their breath when they speak in condemnation of it." This is an exceptional utterance for a US president, whose primary duty it is to honor Rule 12. The "power" he refers to I call *the orthocracy.*

Although no well organized orthocracy allows the rules of rule be made explicit, one can infer the outlines of a *ruling system* behind the veil. One can make such inferences from direct experience (sometimes painful), from direct observation, from meditation on the daily news, or even from introspection, because, like it or not, you *are* the system.

Above all, in order to know the ruling system, one relies upon inference, or deduction. The layman – if he can free himself from political prejudice, which is a big *if* in a system that promotes tenacious belief – may look above, like the astronomer, and observe a firmament of ruling actions day to day. From this body of observation, he may proceed to deduce a pattern of rule consistent with observed behavior. Although there could be other coordinating analogies, I have attempted here to express that pattern in terms of rules. What are the Rules of Rule? There are many imaginable literary ways to go at this subject. I have chosen to create a personification of the orthocracy and to set him talking upon his hallowed Rules.

In this inquiry, the layman has the edge. Any formal academic education in the social sciences may only be an impediment to insight. You will find none of this information in the illusory world of Poly-Sci 101.

Orthocracy Speaks is about the *what* of the system, not the *who* of it. (That has been done well by May Brussels, David Emory, Gary Allen, Jim Marrs, David Ikes, Alex Jones, and many others; thank you, all.) When a proper name appears here it is symbolic or iconic.

If you think conspiratorially, you may want to identify the ruling system with the Illuminati. If you think progressively, you may want to identify the ruling system with a wealthy elite. This book, however, views the system as something far more pervasive.

In my analysis I count thirteen rules of rule. Do they ring a bell? The 13 rules are stated below and they are reiterated throughout the main text in a running foot.

On consideration, you may posit more, or maybe fewer rules, or you may imagine an entirely different way to analyze the system. The field is wide open. It is a vast, unexplored territory, and there are many analytical ways to travel in it. I offer some suggestive evidence to support my analysis. You may think of some even more telling manifestations of the ruling system in action. Once one launches into such an inquiry, supporting evidence seems to be everywhere and inexhaustible.

Here are the thirteen rules, as channeled to me by Orthocracy himself:

The 13 Rules of Rule

1. Keep them weak.
2. Keep them dumb.
3. Keep them scared.
4. Control all resources.
5. Divide and conquer.
6. Control their rhythm and pace.
7. Control their chemistry.
8. Control their sex.
9. Jack them around.
10. Use coercion routinely, brute force when necessary.
11. Use deception routinely, the Big Lie when necessary.
12. None of this can show.
13. This is the system; there shall be no other.

About this word, this neologism, "orthocracy": we speak of the ruling system or *the system*, but the word *system* is vague. *Merriam's 3rd* lists thirteen definitions. I offer instead *orthocracy*, meaning, from the Greek, straight-rule. Think of the colloquial connotations of *straight* (orthodox, uptight). You won't find this neologism in Merriam's or Wikipedia, but *orthocracy* is not absolutely my own coinage; I heard it "in the streets" a few times back in the 1970's, when it may have had some currency.

If you google *orthocracy*, you will be sent to a 1915 tract called *The Orthocratic State.* That must be a publisher's title, because the term is never defined, nor does it ever appear in the text.

As to the historical genesis of the orthocracy, I do not know, but you are welcome to speculate. Is it solely the work of man? Was it created by historical happenstance? Or did it descend by some agency from Jupiter or Mars? I do not know. The orthocracy does seem so alien. Perhaps the orthocracy came straight from Hell. Perhaps this hellish system is a necessary condition of human existence on this earthly plane, which may have a purgatorial purpose.

You might say that this book is Orthocracy's confession, although he shows no contrition. What you make of the esoteric knowledge channeled herein is up to you. Some may make this guide a premise for anarchy or a manifesto for social revolution.

The shrewd may make of it a manual for success.

When I was a clueless college sophomore (at Colgate University in 1957) a half-dozen juniors, poly-sci majors, left campus for a semester as a special study group to Washington, DC. Included were friends Wally and Bill, who, upon their return to campus, reported to fellow students (but probably not to their professors) the esoteric fundamental they had learned down in the nation's capitol, which was, "all of Washington runs on the *sleaze*." This word gained a certain traction in the campus vocabulary, where also current were *snow,* as in "snow job," and *smooth,* meaning slick but tweedy.

Wally and Bill had discovered Rules 11 and 12, and maybe a few more. They were not only amused but thrilled with their new knowledge. What could be accomplished out in the real world via the sleaze?

Bill announced that he was going to sleaze his way into the presidency of our fraternity, was next seen glad-handing brothers in the dining hall, promising god-knows-what, and he won. Then both announced that they were going to sleaze their way into law school. This would be accomplished smoothly by snowing certain key professors in order to secure glowing recommendations. Thus Wally sleazed his way into Harvard Law, Bill into Yale. I'm sure both have had illustrious careers in the orthocracy. The alumni news has Wally yachting in the Bahamas. Knowledge is power.

My own direct experience in the orthocracy, simplified and defined strictly institutionally, includes nine years of Public School, three of Prep, four years drinking my way through the aforementioned College, plus two of Grad School (NYU). This was followed by a dozen years of Corporation. No Military. (It would have been a disaster.) Also about a score of years cumulatively in one or another Marriage of varying degrees of orthocratic intensity.

I never felt adequately "adjusted" in any of these orthocratic institutions. My participation in them always had a compulsory feel.

My direct experience with the institution of Prison, an orthocratic archetype about which I've always been curious, includes only a week or two, cumulatively, for one or another civil-disobedience protest (including two years on federal probation for one of those actions), but my limited prison experience was very revealing.

That's my official orthocratic experience. You?

I retired myself from the direct, continuous grip of orthocratic institutions at age 35. This disengagement was no less than a rebirth, and one dividend was a refreshed perspective on the system. The ideas in this book have been stirring in me for many years since. I write this, finally, in my seventies.

"Retired at 35," I boast. But one can never fully retire from the ubiquitous grip of the orthocracy, not on this earthly plane. Even to fight the system, one seems inevitably to embrace it. But one can lose enthusiasm for the orthocracy, and one can choose deliberately not to honor it and to free oneself from its programs. This is a sensitive and vulnerable position considering the subtle intrusive powers of a well developed orthocracy determined to take over one's very being and able to sneak into one's life under many seductive disguises.

If you are not assiduously true to the anarchist struggling to breathe within you, the orthocracy will digest you.

We elders speak of the old days when "things were better." This is not a senile delusion. We are just appreciating orthocracy's progress over the decades.

This book is one writer's attempt to give a voice to the unspeakable philosophy of the ruling system. If Orthocracy could speak, he might speak like this:

Part One:
Roll Over, Machiavelli

PLEASE ALLOW ME TO INTRODUCE MYSELF. You have no name for me, so I must name myself. I am "The Orthocracy." You have in your language no name for me because I do not let you see me. I rule by a set of rules that cannot be spoken, for, not only is it taboo to voice them, but they are too revolting, too embarrassing for your delicate human sensibilities to bear.

As you see, one of my rules, Rule 12, absolutely prohibits any acknowledgment that such a set of rules even exists. You are, of course, aware that a system of laws, a legal system, exists, but by no means does this system define me, the orthocracy.

So why today, after centuries of diligent silence, do I break the hallowed Rule 12 and allow this confession?

I am old. I am weary. I am bored. And I am smug. This confession is just a little experiment for my own amusement. And where is the risk? If the emperor took off all of his clothes, do you think anyone would notice?

I know the human sensibility well enough to predict how disgusting some of you humans will find these revelations, how your refined sensibilities will evade them and deny them, and how you will want to shoot any messenger who brings you this news.

I do appreciate that knowledge of the secret rules of my orthocracy could, if taken seriously, feed

---

The 13 Rules: 1. Keep them weak. **2.** Keep them dumb. **3.** Keep them scared. **4.** Control all their resources. **5.** Divide and conquer. **6.** Control their rhythm and pace. **7.** Control their chemistry. **8.** Control their sex. **9.** Jack them around. **10.** Use coercion routinely, brute force when necessary. **11.** Use deception routinely, the Big Lie when necessary. **12.** None of this can show. **13.** This is The System, there shall be no other.

humanity's spirit in survival, in revolution, and in transcendence. But it's my bet that the reader will use such knowledge intelligently and make of this book a how-to manual for worldly orthocratic success. Of course, a cynical consciousness of how the world really works gives one an advantage over the naive.

So what is the risk of this confession? Would any respectable book publisher dare to allow the propagation of these truths? Of course not. To do so would violate any publishing corporation's proper orthocratic mission. That is why I have made arrangements with George Trinkaus, a humble independent publisher, to be my channel, my author, my voice, my Editor.

Editor George: *Thank you for that recognition, oh powerful one. May I ask, in compensation for my thankless labors, that I have the privilege of making an occasional inter-locution?*

Granted. But please keep your editorial remarks brief and in italics.

Thank you. I am glad we are finally getting on with this. Your voice has been haunting me for thirty-five years.

Continuing, then, with my exposition:

The 13 Rules: 1. Keep them weak. **2.** Keep them dumb, **3.** Keep them scared. **4.** Control all their resources. **5.** Divide and conquer. **6.** Control their rhythm and pace. **7.** Control their chemistry. **8.** Control their sex. **9.** Jack them around. **10.** Use coercion routinely, brute force when necessary. **11.** Use deception routinely, the Big Lie when necessary. **12.** None of this can show. **13.** This is The System, there shall be no other.

What you, my subjects, call *politics* could be defined as humanity's debate on how to rule. But, even in the narrow ethos of the politicized, the rules of rule cannot be openly discussed, for that would offend the prevailing etiquette, which has been nicely engineered by me. Such candor would be considered impolite, un-politic. This is just one of my many entertaining ironies. Under correct orthocratic conditions, any discourse that could reveal the truth of rule becomes impossible.

The few of you who do attempt some political discourse amuse me with your evasions and circumlocutions. For example, your various isms, this insulting nebulous naming of me: *capitalism, socialism, communism, fascism...* And your *democracy*, ridiculous. Haven't you noticed that however you vote, you always elect me? You pretend that these categories can explain all and that they refer to distinct and competing systems of rule. But in practice all your different isms share the same underlying unutterable rules of rule. Thus your societies function about the same under one ism as under another, that is, under my thumb.

You say some societies are more *totalitarian*, *authoritarian*, etc. What you call *authoritarianism* is just orthocracy taken very seriously. *Paternalism,* ditto. (But I will allow that orthocracy *is* paternal. I am your father.) What you call *imperialism* is orthocracy

---

The 13 Rules: 1. Keep them weak. **2.** Keep them dumb, **3.** Keep them scared. **4.** Control all their resources. **5.** Divide and conquer. **6.** Control their rhythm and pace. **7.** Control their chemistry. **8.** Control their sex. **9.** Jack them around. **10.** Use coercion routinely, brute force when necessary. **11.** Use deception routinely, the Big Lie when necessary. **12.** None of this can show. **13.** This is The System, there shall be no other.

on the march. What you call *fascism* is just me, the orthocracy, in high gear.

That is also a good definition of *war*. War is just me, the orthocracy, in high gear. The rules of rule are the rules of warfare, low-intensity or flat-out. War is orthocracy in celebration.

So war is systemic, and Orthocracy will never give peace a chance?

Indeed, Editor George. "Peace?" I would have difficulty defining that term. It has no place in my system. Please understand that, in order to enforce the orthocratic order, from time to time the extremes of Rule 10 must be activated, and, simultaneously, all of the other rules get cranked up to the max. Peruse the list of Rules. In war they all enjoy a peak intensity. Yes, I go to war in order to enforce the order, but also to expand the order, to reorder the order, or maybe just for the hell of it.

Blood flows, and this is what you call your World War II, your War on Terror, and so forth.

For such high occasions, I can always find among the masses plenty of volunteers for the blood sacrifice. And always available is some zealous orthocrat to lead your government into war. When, in retrospect, you demonize your Hitler, your Mussolini, your Bush, or whatever wartime dictator, when you enshrine these

---

The 13 Rules: 1. Keep them weak. **2.** Keep them dumb, **3.** Keep them scared. **4.** Control all their resources. **5.** Divide and conquer. **6.** Control their rhythm and pace. **7.** Control their chemistry. **8.** Control their sex. **9.** Jack them around. **10.** Use coercion routinely, brute force when necessary. **11.** Use deception routinely, the Big Lie when necessary. **12.** None of this can show. **13.** This is The System, there shall be no other.

personalities in your histories and elevate them to apotheoses of evil, I am amused, for they were only my servants of the moment.

the orthocratic personality

I'm talking here about the product, *You*. There are, of course, varying degrees of success in my programming, varying degrees of orthocraticism in the final product, varying degrees of enthusiasm and honor for me, the system.

There is the enthusiast, the orthocracy-religious. He usually gets the message young and is hard-wired to my ways from early on. He is identifiable as a candidate for my priesthood even as a schoolboy and may get tapped when he is an undergrad. He may become one of the orthocratic elite, one of the official leadership, and there can only be a few.

Affluence follows the gradient I am laying out here.

The immediate sub-elite is a swarm of junior-enthusiasts. Today's ideal is young, ambitious, short-haired, dark-suited, English-speaking, cute, perky, and white.

But I take nearly equal satisfaction in the production of a sub-elite class of less zealous personality who may not be so deeply wedded to my ways (may even secretly be a bit dissident), but who has put himself

The 13 Rules: 1. Keep them weak. **2.** Keep them dumb, **3.** Keep them scared. **4.** Control all their resources. **5.** Divide and conquer. **6.** Control their rhythm and pace. **7.** Control their chemistry. **8.** Control their sex. **9.** Jack them around. **10.** Use coercion routinely, brute force when necessary. **11.** Use deception routinely, the Big Lie when necessary. **12.** None of this can show. **13.** This is The System, there shall be no other.

in orthocratic employment, is sufficiently submissive to his managers to be functional and to contribute to the orthocracy, dissidence notwithstanding. He, too, ultimately is mine.

Then there is the unenthusiast. Merely orthocracy-tolerant, he gets along by going along. He is in the underclass, often the "working" class. He lives in envy of the higher orthocrats that he hates. I may never win his enthusiasm, but ultimately he is mine.

Descending downward, there is the overt dissident, who, though disgusted with the orthocracy in all of its manifestations, still lurks impecuniously and dependently around its edges, minimally cooperative. I have orthocratized fashion modes to channel safely his discontent, so, in an oblique way, I have a grip on him, too.

Finally, for the unredeemable resistor there are my prisons, my whips, chains, and nooses (Rule 10).

desired characteristics in my product

Personality production is still an unpredictable and haphazard process. The triumph of genetic engineering will be *homo orthocratis.* Desired above all is predictability. No surprises, please. Orthocracy is tolerant of multifarious styles, but I insist on adherence to approved orthocratic patterns which are predictable.

The 13 Rules: 1. Keep them weak. **2.** Keep them dumb. **3.** Keep them scared. **4.** Control all their resources. **5.** Divide and conquer. **6.** Control their rhythm and pace. **7.** Control their chemistry. **8.** Control their sex. **9.** Jack them around. **10.** Use coercion routinely, brute force when necessary. **11.** Use deception routinely, the Big Lie when necessary. **12.** None of this can show. **13.** This is The System, there shall be no other.

Unfortunately, it is necessary that novel patterns be continually introduced on the cultural surface in order to relieve orthocratic ennui.

Novelty does not come easily. I, the orthocracy, would prefer to be the sole progenitor of any new style – behavioral, linguistic, musical, choreographic, sartorial, whatever – but, since I have no culture or original creativity of my own (I do admit this; and I'll admit also that I am boring), I must observe style as it arises spontaneously from indigenous, or dissident, or otherwise non-orthocratic cultures, take ownership of style as my own resource (Rule 4), including so-called *lifestyle*, redefine style, and then propagate the redefinition through my mass media (Rules 2 and 11), thus bending the errant culture to my own orthocratic purposes, which would include the exercise of Rules 6, 7, and 8. Still with me?

Once co-opted into the orthocracy, the novel style can be highly differentiated. That is, the style can be cool to some subcultures but outrageous to others, thus serving Rule 5. That takes creativity of a Madison-Avenue sort.

Orthocracy's model product is not necessarily standardized to the straight-arrow, the jock, or the Babbitt. A well developed modern orthocracy encourages a product diversity, a multiplicity of conformities that meet orthocratic standards of predictability.

The 13 Rules: 1. Keep them weak. **2.** Keep them dumb. **3.** Keep them scared. **4.** Control all their resources. **5.** Divide and conquer. **6.** Control their rhythm and pace. **7.** Control their chemistry. **8.** Control their sex. **9.** Jack them around. **10.** Use coercion routinely, brute force when necessary. **11.** Use deception routinely, the Big Lie when necessary. **12.** None of this can show. **13.** This is The System, there shall be no other.

These conformities ideally have frictional social relationships with one another, and maybe outright hostilities can be arranged (Rule 5 again, of course).

When dealing with those deviant non-orthocratic cultures from which style must be drawn, Orthocracy takes a risk. The normally desired predictability must be sacrificed. It is always experimental.

Experimentation begins with cliché probes. The clichés and the associated talent, if the probe catches on, get visibility and other empowerments. But orthocratic powers conferred upon the unpredictable can be misused. From time to time it may be necessary to eliminate a Hendrix, a Joplin, a Lennon. Unwanted trends can develop. But from any emerging subcultural phenomenon that could develop unpredictably, orthocracy can contrive a parallel synthetic phenomenon that is properly controlled and propagate it on a massive scale.

So out of spontaneous music comes Muzak?

Yes, that and beautiful-music, disco, lite-jazz, Jesus rock — all sorts of programmed music, including always the orthocratically constrained "popular" music — all of these genres propagated by megawatts, mega-pressings, and file-sharings.

I think there may be literary equivalents.

The 13 Rules: 1. Keep them weak. **2.** Keep them dumb, **3.** Keep them scared. **4.** Control all their resources. **5.** Divide and conquer. **6.** Control their rhythm and pace. **7.** Control their chemistry. **8.** Control their sex. **9.** Jack them around. **10.** Use coercion routinely, brute force when necessary. **11.** Use deception routinely, the Big Lie when necessary. **12.** None of this can show. **13.** This is The System, there shall be no other.

Of course, and incidentally they will function to render our literary work here safely invisible. For example, the mass production of popular and genre fiction — sci-fi, detective, western, romance, and so forth — churning continuously off high-speed web presses in print runs of hundreds of thousands.

There sure is a lot of fiction published.

It is important to instill in the consciousness of the masses a habit of suspending disbelief. Consider Rule 11 and Rule 12.

Nonfiction has its genres, too, and anyway my publishers turn out a hundred thousand new book titles every year, effectively glutting the market in order to control it.

So true. Who would know my industry better than you. But you are rubbing it in, Orthocracy. That hurts… Anyway, onward: "synthesizing subcultures," you were saying?

Yes, I was boasting how synthetic orthocratic culture-constructs can be cogently propagated through media and educational orthocracies.

But then, Orthocracy, if this idea is taken to its logical conclusion, you might boast that a cultural bubble could be synthesized that is all-embracing, a real-world Disneyland.

The 13 Rules: 1. Keep them weak. **2.** Keep them dumb. **3.** Keep them scared. **4.** Control all their resources. **5.** Divide and conquer. **6.** Control their rhythm and pace. **7.** Control their chemistry. **8.** Control their sex. **9.** Jack them around. **10.** Use coercion routinely, brute force when necessary. **11.** Use deception routinely, the Big Lie when necessary. **12.** None of this can show. **13.** This is The System, there shall be no other.

Yes indeed, synthesized and imposed. I sponsor many bubbles of consciousness. Often they are set against each other (Rule 5). The process is well underway particularly in your USA, George.

But why "my" USA in particular?

Compared to many places on your planet with more rooted cultures, the USA was a *tabla rasa,* a cultural clean slate to write an orthocracy upon. Of course I mean after those aboriginal cultures had been erased and the land had been re-populated by descendants of established European orthocracies.

I permeate everything.

Orthocracy permeates all of what you call "the civilized world." Orthocracy is civilization. Civilization is orthocracy. My rules of rule are routinely exercised and perpetuated by various institutional entities of civilization which are charged, overtly or tacitly (mostly tacitly), with doing the job. These include, not only your institutions of government, but those of business and the workplace, of religion, of media, of schooling, of the family, and of the institutionalized, orthocratized You.

Orthocracy resides, secretly, not only among those elite true-believers that wield it most, but within you all. It governs your behavior, public or

---

The 13 Rules: 1. Keep them weak. **2.** Keep them dumb, **3.** Keep them scared. **4.** Control all their resources. **5.** Divide and conquer. **6.** Control their rhythm and pace. **7.** Control their chemistry. **8.** Control their sex. **9.** Jack them around. **10.** Use coercion routinely, brute force when necessary. **11.** Use deception routinely, the Big Lie when necessary. **12.** None of this can show. **13.** This is The System, there shall be no other.

intimate, day to day. You routinely honor me, either in exercising my rules over others or in submitting to them yourselves.

I permeate all and I will persist forever. I am the Thousand-year Reich (Rule 13). I rule even the elites that rule. CEO, I am your heart attack.

Please appreciate that my most passionate and devoted followers, those orthocratic true-believers (whom you might call the orthocracy-religious), it is they who constitute the so-called elite, and it is they who may be the most ruled of all — and suffer accordingly.

I am the true environmentalist.
The society that you take for granted is an orthocratic work. Your society, your "environment," to use the fashionable term, is a studiously designed product of my senior architects. Your day-to-day civilized landscape is my craft. The well-paid professionals who are the architects of orthocratic rule: you can thank them for your freeways and for the engineering of the cars that you mindlessly run on them, for your supermarkets, your shopping malls, your housing tracts, your own habitat's design, the design of your office or factory, your industrial parks, your theme parks, your theme restaurants, your urban condos and office towers, and, of course, the programming of your ubiquitous television.

The 13 Rules: 1. Keep them weak. **2.** Keep them dumb. **3.** Keep them scared. **4.** Control all their resources. **5.** Divide and conquer. **6.** Control their rhythm and pace. **7.** Control their chemistry. **8.** Control their sex. **9.** Jack them around. **10.** Use coercion routinely, brute force when necessary. **11.** Use deception routinely, the Big Lie when necessary. **12.** None of this can show. **13.** This is The System, there shall be no other.

Your civilized world is the work of my environmentalism. I am the true environmentalist. Civilization, your dominant environment, is my own construct. Civilization is the orthocracy materialized.

I am the true progressive.

I, the orthocracy, have a life and will of my own. And I have a decisive direction of development. I am the true progressive. I move naturally, inexorably, and progressively towards a utopia of total planetary rule. *Totalitarianism* and *globalism* are words you use for this ideal orthocratic condition on those few occasions when you dare to discuss the matter.

Those partisan sentimentalists who call themselves "progressives" entertain a 500-year plan, but their social-justice utopia is forever receding, as mine expands. Orthocratic progress is laid out in 50-year plans that do come to fruition.

Every deed that you do in the name of any of my rules, whether done actively or submissively, reinforces and perpetuates my power, at the expense of yours.

I have a million subtle ways. I wear many disguises, and when I take you over, you will not even know it. If I can, I will get you as a child. By the time you declare adulthood, I usually have you in my grasp and any exorcism is unlikely. Your fragile human spirit may struggle to survive

---

The 13 Rules: 1. Keep them weak. **2.** Keep them dumb, **3.** Keep them scared. **4.** Control all their resources. **5.** Divide and conquer. **6.** Control their rhythm and pace. **7.** Control their chemistry. **8.** Control their sex. **9.** Jack them around. **10.** Use coercion routinely, brute force when necessary. **11.** Use deception routinely, the Big Lie when necessary. **12.** None of this can show. **13.** This is The System, there shall be no other.

against orthocracy. Spontaneous spiritual energy is an anarchy threatening to orthocracy. What you romance as "free spirit" must be tortured and crushed into orthocratic churchy conformities. But you may be quite peacefully taken over. The orthocracy has its noisy torturing side, but it also has its quiet, seductive side.

I am the true religion.

The hollow men of religion make some of my very best workers. They say they are working for the Lord. Well, who's that? I, the orthocracy, may be immaterial, but I am a living entity, a living deity, a living force. I am transcendently and indifferently separate from humanity and its petty day-to-day self-interests.

About my separate existence. Please understand that, being independent and life-transcendent, I am self-sustained by my own physics and chemistry, and my behavior is regulated by my own immutable laws (the rules of rule, of course). My pristine existence is far above messy human motivation or will. Appreciate my mission, and that is control of the citizenry of the world, control unto predictability, control unto domestication, control unto slavery, control unto death. I am the ultimate control freak. Control is my reason for being.

The 13 Rules: 1. Keep them weak. **2.** Keep them dumb. **3.** Keep them scared. **4.** Control all their resources. **5.** Divide and conquer. **6.** Control their rhythm and pace. **7.** Control their chemistry. **8.** Control their sex. **9.** Jack them around. **10.** Use coercion routinely, brute force when necessary. **11.** Use deception routinely, the Big Lie when necessary. **12.** None of this can show. **13.** This is The System, there shall be no other.

Do not expect me ever to serve human interests. To me humanity is just a management problem. Do not expect my sympathy for any of your worldly pains that may result from my orthocratic assertions. This is one of your prime delusions, that my incarnations, in such forms as governments or corporations or churches, are here to help you and will respond to your petitions, appeals, and lamentations. This notion I must promote as part of my perennial cover-up (Rule 12). In reality, to maintain the orthocratic order, there is some very ugly work that I must do. Expect no human sympathy from me. I may be bombing your neighborhood tomorrow.

Call me an evil god. Call me satanic. Call me demonic. I have no feelings, only intelligence. Of your suffering I have not a care. And I know how to teach my faithful not to care.

Institutionalized.

Any spontaneous cooperative activity among you in the name of the commercial, the social, the familial, the political, the spiritual, however innocently conceived, tends naturally to coagulate around my ruling ways and eventually becomes institutionalized into some agency or defender of my orthocratic interests. This orthocratic permeation will happen always everywhere with any organized

---

The 13 Rules: 1. Keep them weak. **2.** Keep them dumb, **3.** Keep them scared. **4.** Control all their resources. **5.** Divide and conquer. **6.** Control their rhythm and pace. **7.** Control their chemistry. **8.** Control their sex. **9.** Jack them around. **10.** Use coercion routinely, brute force when necessary. **11.** Use deception routinely, the Big Lie when necessary. **12.** None of this can show. **13.** This is The System, there shall be no other.

group, unless a very special vigilance is exercised, which, fortunately, is rarely the case.

You invent an alphabet of governmental agencies to defend you: DOD, EPA, SEC, FDA, DEA, ATF, FEMA, NRC, FCC. Then you show amazement when these institutional creations turn on you. But they are just performing according to their respective orthocratic missions. They are also going through many excruciating contortions, in honor of Rule 12, to look like, and actually believe like, they are doing something utterly different from their true orthocratic functions.

This is true of all workers in orthocratic industry as well as in government. You, who are employed and clock-watching in the system anywhere at whatever level must know this. I know you know it.

It's the money, you say?

When you bother to analyze me at all, you like to argue that money drives the system. Yes, I reward my cooperators with a living. I reward my non-cooperators with a nonliving. Those who honor me religiously and those who wield my system over the masses, I honor them with wealth. It is a truth that the deeper you get into money the more you become mine, and visa-versa. Money is about coercion (Rule 10) and little else. That the buck stops here with me is a truth of economics forbidden by Rule 12.

The 13 Rules: 1. Keep them weak. **2.** Keep them dumb, **3.** Keep them scared. **4.** Control all their resources. **5.** Divide and conquer. **6.** Control their rhythm and pace. **7.** Control their chemistry. **8.** Control their sex. **9.** Jack them around. **10.** Use coercion routinely, brute force when necessary. **11.** Use deception routinely, the Big Lie when necessary. **12.** None of this can show. **13.** This is The System, there shall be no other.

However, it is not money that drives orthocracy. Money may circulate like blood in the orthocracy, but it does not drive me.

Money is just the oil of the orthocratic system (and, as a matter of fact, oil, the hydrocarbon product, functions like money in the system). Oh, it may be useful in deciphering my ways to "follow the money," as you say, but then you will only see some of my veins. My true physiology and anatomy will continue to elude you.

Roll over Dr. Nietzsche

You also like to argue that what drives the system is the human passion to control others, *the will to power*. Yes, that passion in you is much exploited by me. But please understand that, once institutionalized, orthocracy takes on a life all of its own. Orthocracy may entrain will, but the orthocracy does not exist in the aggregate will of a class of greedy capitalists. That is another Rule-12 myth.

> *But, when you say that money does not drive the system, you are upsetting the dominant paradigm of Left politics.*

I am the dominant paradigm.

A hallowed political philosophy would crumble if this truth were to breach Rule 12 and enter

---

The 13 Rules: 1. Keep them weak. **2.** Keep them dumb. **3.** Keep them scared. **4.** Control all their resources. **5.** Divide and conquer. **6.** Control their rhythm and pace. **7.** Control their chemistry. **8.** Control their sex. **9.** Jack them around. **10.** Use coercion routinely, brute force when necessary. **11.** Use deception routinely, the Big Lie when necessary. **12.** None of this can show. **13.** This is The System, there shall be no other.

human consciousness. My academics must remain committed to the perpetuation of the fat-capitalist theory — or else. This is Rule-10 coercion applied at the university level in the name of maintaining Rule-13, which is a fundamental duty of the educator.

And, to cite another of your rules, you seem to be saying, in contradiction to popular wisdom, that the orthocratic educator is a maintainer of Rule 2.

Correct. You are learning, George.

conspiratorial?

The more perspicacious among you see many conspiracies in the workings of orthocratic institutions. Are you beginning to see why conspiracy is necessary and inevitable in my system and why the conspiracy-theorist must always be silenced? Rule 12 rules. I am the "They," and I am the "Who-benefits" of all conspiracies.

Excuse me, Orthocracy, but what you are laying out here might be called "the ultimate conspiracy theory."

You have a point there, Editor George, and a book-cover blurb.

The 13 Rules: 1. Keep them weak. **2.** Keep them dumb. **3.** Keep them scared. **4.** Control all their resources. **5.** Divide and conquer. **6.** Control their rhythm and pace. **7.** Control their chemistry. **8.** Control their sex. **9.** Jack them around. **10.** Use coercion routinely, brute force when necessary. **11.** Use deception routinely, the Big Lie when necessary. **12.** None of this can show. **13.** This is The System, there shall be no other.

criminal?

You complain that your politicians, once they are elected and safely inside official orthocratic government, inevitably become "corrupt" and cease to represent your interests. That is because they inevitably become dedicated to my rules of rule. The same goes for all of the leaders of all of your orthocratic institutions: your corporate CEO's and their executive minions, your educators, your foundation directors, your churchmen, doctors, lawyers, labor leaders, journalists, broadcasters, publishers. They are all mine. Know my rules, know their world.

You continuously complain that your leaders become liars and hypocrites. Are you beginning to see why this is inevitable? You go cluck, cluck with your tongue and wave your finger. Oh, they are lawless criminals! Yes, they are breakers of your written law. But, if anyone wrote the law for the system as it is, nobody would accept it. Who would ratify a constitution that read like the thirteen rules of rule? Yet this is the operative constitution in every established orthocracy on the planet.

Whew! The word for this is "Machiavellian", but you leave Machiavelli in the dust!

"Machiavellian," you say? *The Prince* is just a bedtime story for children. Roll over, Machiavelli!

The 13 Rules: 1. Keep them weak. **2.** Keep them dumb, **3.** Keep them scared. **4.** Control all their resources. **5.** Divide and conquer. **6.** Control their rhythm and pace. **7.** Control their chemistry. **8.** Control their sex. **9.** Jack them around. **10.** Use coercion routinely, brute force when necessary. **11.** Use deception routinely, the Big Lie when necessary. **12.** None of this can show. **13.** This is The System, there shall be no other.

You were just scratching the surface of my system as it was back in your time. And look how far I have brought this game today!

The 13 Rules: 1. Keep them weak. **2.** Keep them dumb, **3.** Keep them scared. **4.** Control all their resources. **5.** Divide and conquer. **6.** Control their rhythm and pace. **7.** Control their chemistry. **8.** Control their sex. **9.** Jack them around. **10.** Use coercion routinely, brute force when necessary. **11.** Use deception routinely, the Big Lie when necessary. **12.** None of this can show. **13.** This is The System, there shall be no other.

Part Two:
Orthocracy Parses the 13 Rules of Rule

THAT WAS A PASSIONATE EXPOSITION, Orthocracy. It is evident that you have much to get off your chest. Perhaps you could further explicate one-by-one the thirteen rules of rule for our readers.

"Explicate." Such a vocabulary, Editor George. As a matter of fact, my social-science orthocrats could explicate this work exhaustively, if they dared to give it any notice. Yes, perhaps if I just briefly articulated the outlines of the rules one-by-one.

Rule 1. Keep them weak.

You may wonder why "keep them weak" is rule number one. Peruse the Rules of Rule, and see how all of the other rules harmonize with, and abet, Rule 1. Your intellectuals, however, would elevate to the top Rule 10, insisting that my rule is by "thugs with guns." This is an insulting observation. In recent centuries, my rule has become considerably more subtle and sophisticated, and the Rule-10 technologies of coercion themselves have become considerably more refined and subtle as they have become more pervasive and persuasive.

Keep them weak? Yes, debilitation must be nurtured. A stable orthocracy must not have a robust population. A well developed orthocracy enshrines debilitation and institutionalizes it into an organized

---

The 13 Rules: 1. Keep them weak. **2.** Keep them dumb. **3.** Keep them scared. **4.** Control all their resources. **5.** Divide and conquer. **6.** Control their rhythm and pace. **7.** Control their chemistry. **8.** Control their sex. **9.** Jack them around. **10.** Use coercion routinely, brute force when necessary. **11.** Use deception routinely, the Big Lie when necessary. **12.** None of this can show. **13.** This is The System, there shall be no other.

medicine, which, in the spirit of Rule 4, takes exclusive custody of all of society's healing powers, thus defining the limits of general health. Health is an orthocratic matter. It has long been the domain of government and other orthocracies. You might say that health is another resource to be managed under Rule 4.

You must love Obamacare.

The management of orthocratic medicine can only be enhanced under the thumb of governmental orthocracies in combination with the corporate. The medical orthocracy endorses a debilitating diet. The medical orthocracy embraces the pharmaceutical one and opens up many direct vectors of incapacitation through chemistry (Rule 7).

Orthocratic vectors of incapacitation can be environmental, but appreciate that through orthocratic medicine I can get directly into the bodies of my subjects by topical application, pill, syringe, scalpel, or irradiation. Finally orthocratic medicine knows how to ease its patients into an early death in a relatively painless stupefied state (Rule 7). Modern orthocratic medicine welds the individual to a powerful orthocratic institution from birth to death. It is one of my highest accomplishments.

As a senior citizen, observing his peers in their premature disablement and demise, I can vouch for that.

The 13 Rules: 1. Keep them weak. **2.** Keep them dumb, **3.** Keep them scared. **4.** Control all their resources. **5.** Divide and conquer. **6.** Control their rhythm and pace. **7.** Control their chemistry. **8.** Control their sex. **9.** Jack them around. **10.** Use coercion routinely, brute force when necessary. **11.** Use deception routinely, the Big Lie when necessary. **12.** None of this can show. **13.** This is The System, there shall be no other.

Be clear about the human capacities that particularly must be incapacitated under Rule 1. They are the ones that could threaten my order. Appreciate therefore that life-energy itself must be properly regulated. Consider life-energy to be just another resource to be managed under Rule 4.

A broad interpretation of Rule 4, indeed, orthocracy. Your managerial reach knows no limits.

Another example, Editor George: The modern orthocracy can take for granted that most of its adults are held securely in employment by powerful institutions that tell them when to get up in the morning, and thus own their day (except on weekends, when they are sent out shopping). No one holds a gun to their heads. The orthocratic activity called employment is so normal that to refrain is abnormal. The employed are firmly under control and their energies drained from 9:00 to 5:00, or 8:00 to 6:00, or 7:00 to 7:00, or whatever the expanding workday is now. And don't forget to count the hours of commuting. The exhaustion of the workday is a normal condition that nicely fulfills Rule 1.

Employment is a fundamental orthocratic institution that facilitates the exercise of many of the Rules. For example, the rhythms of employment are the great enforcer of Rule 6. The employment

---

The 13 Rules: 1. Keep them weak. **2.** Keep them dumb, **3.** Keep them scared. **4.** Control all their resources. **5.** Divide and conquer. **6.** Control their rhythm and pace. **7.** Control their chemistry. **8.** Control their sex. **9.** Jack them around. **10.** Use coercion routinely, brute force when necessary. **11.** Use deception routinely, the Big Lie when necessary. **12.** None of this can show. **13.** This is The System, there shall be no other.

situation opens unlimited possibilities for the exercise of Rule 9. And so forth.

Encouraged by pragmatic materialism, the condition of employment is taken for granted as if it were an existential inevitable. Also consider all the positive sentiment that can be attached, the romancing of Labor, of Work, and of the almighty Job. The establishment of this human condition is celebrated by historians as The Industrial Revolution. It is a great orthocratic triumph, if you think about it, but nobody does.

What about the condition of unemployment?

It is a counter-condition. It exists only in the context of employment. It is an orthocratic sub-institution with its own orthocratic disciplines. Unemployment insurance, for example, opens many Rule-9 opportunities. A consequence of unemployment can be enforced poverty, which has a long orthocratic tradition.

Indeed it is true that many continue to be held in impotence by grinding poverty. Rule by ugly deprivation (Rule 4), generally accompanied by tight policing (Rule 10), may have been the dominant mode of disabling the roiling masses, but please appreciate how today's orthocracy can develop an equally subdued population couched in comfort and even luxury.

The 13 Rules: 1. Keep them weak. **2.** Keep them dumb, **3.** Keep them scared. **4.** Control all their resources. **5.** Divide and conquer. **6.** Control their rhythm and pace. **7.** Control their chemistry. **8.** Control their sex. **9.** Jack them around. **10.** Use coercion routinely, brute force when necessary. **11.** Use deception routinely, the Big Lie when necessary. **12.** None of this can show. **13.** This is The System, there shall be no other.

"Couched in comfort and luxury:" That is a description of my USA as I've known it, but today your forces seem to be pushing the society into a third-world deprivation model.

For the USA it is a time for some major adjustments in the orthocratic order.

Continuing more succinctly down the Rules then:

Rule 2. Keep them dumb.

Rule 2 is the circumscribing of consciousness. It is the management of perception, attention, memory, and imagination. Rule 2 is just the intellectual extension of Rule 1. You might consider intellect and consciousness as resources to be regulated in the spirit of Rule 4. Orthocracy will know everything. You will know nothing.

Rule 2 is administered by the orthocratic institutions of schooling, publishing, and broadcasting, which, in a particular era, may be predominantly in the hands of the government, the corporation, or the church. Which orthocracy makes little difference to me.

In respect to the church: Rule 2 triumphs when my existence is unimaginable (Rule 12). Attention must be given to the management of imagination, which is a dangerous faculty. The perception of me

---

The 13 Rules: 1. Keep them weak. **2.** Keep them dumb. **3.** Keep them scared. **4.** Control all their resources. **5.** Divide and conquer. **6.** Control their rhythm and pace. **7.** Control their chemistry. **8.** Control their sex. **9.** Jack them around. **10.** Use coercion routinely, brute force when necessary. **11.** Use deception routinely, the Big Lie when necessary. **12.** None of this can show. **13.** This is The System, there shall be no other.

requires a dark imagination. When the dark side is vanquished, when the imagination is deadened, Rule 2 is fulfilled and Rule 12 benefits. The best religions vanquish the black and paint it all white. Then I become invisible. When it comes to religion, give me the vapid, the insipid, the pale. Nothing too passionate, vivid or deep, please.

Despite Catholicism's great contribution to Rule 2, The Church does not reign supreme in that department, because (in the spirit of Rule 3) the Church conjures demons in the unconscious, which has the unfortunate side-effect of bringing the imagination to life. The awakened imagination may conduct the soul into dangerous occult cultures, like music, art, literature, psychedelics, and conspiracy theory.

But the proper orthocratic Protestant gets his depths erased clean and innocent. His imagination deadened, there can be no dark side. In this smug consciousness, a solid materialism finds a home, and affluence naturally follows. Now I can never be seen. Blinded to me and my ways, If some impolite dissident were to warn of some dark action on my part (one of my Rule-11 Big-Lie deceptions, for example) there would be no hook anywhere in the lobotomized consciousness of the good Lutheran or whatever to hang such an outrageous thought upon: Not in our world, he says. Here everything is basically OK.

The 13 Rules: 1. Keep them weak. **2.** Keep them dumb. **3.** Keep them scared. **4.** Control all their resources. **5.** Divide and conquer. **6.** Control their rhythm and pace. **7.** Control their chemistry. **8.** Control their sex. **9.** Jack them around. **10.** Use coercion routinely, brute force when necessary. **11.** Use deception routinely, the Big Lie when necessary. **12.** None of this can show. **13.** This is The System, there shall be no other.

Sounds like NPR.

Good orthocrats think positively.

Rule 3. Keep them scared.

Appreciate how Rule 3 abets Rule 2, how terror numbs consciousness and enables its management. "When the bombs start falling, all you know is fear," said the Iraqi. Yes, a dose of shock and awe from time to time, but more important is the maintenance of a persistent anxiety. This can be arranged by administering certain social conditions, which is well within the power of certain orthocratic institutions.

Consider, for example, the pervasive institution of driving. This is another daily activity like employment and allied to it. Driving is romanced as a leisure experience. but in reality the driver is just participating in another orthocratic activity. In fact, there is nothing more congenial to the orthocracy than the driving of an automobile.

Hmmm ... What about the activity of computing?

A close competitor. Both engage the consciousness in highly regulated, uptight, yes-no regimes. Both contribute to isolation (Rule 5). Computing may be

---

The 13 Rules: 1. Keep them weak. **2.** Keep them dumb. **3.** Keep them scared. **4.** Control all their resources. **5.** Divide and conquer. **6.** Control their rhythm and pace. **7.** Control their chemistry. **8.** Control their sex. **9.** Jack them around. **10.** Use coercion routinely, brute force when necessary. **11.** Use deception routinely, the Big Lie when necessary. **12.** None of this can show. **13.** This is The System, there shall be no other.

the winner over driving on the jack-around (Rule 9). Computing, like driving, also has its terrors (Rule 3), including the crash. On the road, Rule 3 operates mostly at the subconscious level, which is where orthocracy prefers to work. The typical trip may take the driver to his destination without incident. However, inherent in every trip are sure to be one or more of the following anxieties:

What's that noise? Will this vehicle break down? Will my brakes fail? Can I afford the repairs? Can I pay the next installment? Is that the repo-man following me? Is that a cop following me? Is he doing a make on my plates? Will I get stopped? Are my papers in order? Is my insurance paid up? Will he smell those drinks? Can I pass a Breathalyzer? Will he find my open container? My stash? Will I get arrested, a DUI, bankrupted by fines and fees, go to jail? Will my life be destroyed?

That burning wreak at the side of the road: Can that happen to me?

How depressing if any of the above contingencies were to occur. But psychic depression is a condition of consciousness that orthocracy seeks to nurture. Keep 'em bummed is a sub-rule of Rule 3. Keep 'em scared, yes, but also keep 'em bummed.

The 13 Rules: 1. Keep them weak. **2.** Keep them dumb, **3.** Keep them scared. **4.** Control all their resources. **5.** Divide and conquer. **6.** Control their rhythm and pace. **7.** Control their chemistry. **8.** Control their sex. **9.** Jack them around. **10.** Use coercion routinely, brute force when necessary. **11.** Use deception routinely, the Big Lie when necessary. **12.** None of this can show. **13.** This is The System, there shall be no other.

Rule 4. Control all resources.

This is another rule that fashionable intellectuals would promote up to rule number 1 or 2. Greedy capitalists exploit labor to extract from the planet all of its gold, coal, copper, oil, diamonds, or whatever for personal and corporate profit. The heart of the system is about "profit maximization" and "the bottom line." That is the narrative, and there shall be no other, say all of my respectable academics.

So what is the standard narrative concealing? Please allow the word *resources* a broader definition than the likes of gold or diamonds. Allow the word to embrace certain intangible resources. Human energy, for example. Reference here, please, Rule 1. Understand that I am less about the management of extracted material resources than the management of human energy in all of its manifestations — physiological, spiritual, and even libidinous (Rule 8).

For example, an established European orthocracy successfully insinuates itself into some undeveloped (i.e., under-orthocratized) tribal or peasant territory. Fashion calls this "imperialism." The challenge then becomes: how to domesticate the energies of the population? Extraction is one way, and the product can be sent home to justify the campaign, which actually may have been conducted in the name of Rule 13. It is no longer necessary to mine diamonds in Rhodesia, since warehouses are bursting with

---

The 13 Rules: 1. Keep them weak. **2.** Keep them dumb. **3.** Keep them scared. **4.** Control all their resources. **5.** Divide and conquer. **6.** Control their rhythm and pace. **7.** Control their chemistry. **8.** Control their sex. **9.** Jack them around. **10.** Use coercion routinely, brute force when necessary. **11.** Use deception routinely, the Big Lie when necessary. **12.** None of this can show. **13.** This is The System, there shall be no other.

them in Holland, but the mining must go on, rigorously directing the energies of the natives into an orthocratically congenial process.

Aboriginal societies have been known to function fine on a two-hour workday.

That may be true, but no good orthocrat of an anthropologist would allow that to be known.

Back in the 1950's social scientists were speculating on a future in which man was liberated from employment by automation.

You see how that worked out, orthocratically I mean. Industry is an orthocratic necessity, and it migrates to regions most in need of that particular orthocratic occupation. As a dividend, industrial emissions and effluents may help to degrade various natural resources which the society under revision may have depended upon to sustain its backward existence.

Getting back to Rule 4 and resource-management on the material plane: Appreciate that to me the planet itself is a resource. The managerial challenge is to geo-engineer planet Earth out of the chaos of nature and into a more orthocratically congenial

---

The 13 Rules: 1. Keep them weak. **2.** Keep them dumb, **3.** Keep them scared. **4.** Control all their resources. **5.** Divide and conquer. **6.** Control their rhythm and pace. **7.** Control their chemistry. **8.** Control their sex. **9.** Jack them around. **10.** Use coercion routinely, brute force when necessary. **11.** Use deception routinely, the Big Lie when necessary. **12.** None of this can show. **13.** This is The System, there shall be no other.

global environment (by Rule-7 modalities, for example).

Rule 5. Divide them, conquer them.
Having noticed the tendency of my subjects to root to the land under their feet and to form cohesive little local societies there, I make it my business to disrupt this process, sending them hither and yon in order to bond them to transcendent orthocratic institutions.

Having observed a natural and easy affinity among my subjects, I make it my business to disrupt personal connections generally. It is fashionable to speak of "the community." There are no "communities." There may be demographics, but there are no damn communities.

Having observed a natural inclination to rivalry, I make it my business to encourage this tendency by injecting a wholesome spirit of divisive competition into all of business, schooling, and sport.

I have noticed in my subjects an inclination to make invidious distinctions about each other. Any existing distinction becomes an opportunity for division, so I exaggerate all existing distinctions, as I make up new ones. The well educated orthocrat is astute at making distinctions; he is an astute snob, exquisitely aloof, discerning, and disconnected.

The 13 Rules: 1. Keep them weak. **2.** Keep them dumb. **3.** Keep them scared. **4.** Control all their resources. **5.** Divide and conquer. **6.** Control their rhythm and pace. **7.** Control their chemistry. **8.** Control their sex. **9.** Jack them around. **10.** Use coercion routinely, brute force when necessary. **11.** Use deception routinely, the Big Lie when necessary. **12.** None of this can show. **13.** This is The System, there shall be no other.

What you call *racism* is just the making of a particular distinction. If the distinction is made with no N-words in a benign, liberal context, Rule 5 can operate invisibly, and all the more effectively.

Sounds like NPR again.

That is a great orthocratic institution.

A less subtle Rule-5 instance is Rwanda, where clever Belgian orthocrats arbitrarily split in two the Hutu and the Tutsi, descendants of the same tribe. They were divided according to skin color and other minor distinctions, which were advertised on radio. When the action came down, government-issued identification cards became useful at the checkpoints. Thus, an inconvenient population was efficiently reduced by 800,000 in just 100 days.

To get back to the more routine orthocratics of driving cars: The choice of the orthocracy to remove public transportation and to put the commuter behind the wheel is a Rule-5 planning expedient consistent with the suburban plan, which is a Rule-5 planning expedient in itself. With each privately contained in his own wheeled compartment, traveler is safely divided from fellow traveler. Because traffic congestion prolongs this condition, it is an orthocratic asset, which is why congestion dependably increases but never abates.

The 13 Rules: 1. Keep them weak. **2.** Keep them dumb, **3.** Keep them scared. **4.** Control all their resources. **5.** Divide and conquer. **6.** Control their rhythm and pace. **7.** Control their chemistry. **8.** Control their sex. **9.** Jack them around. **10.** Use coercion routinely, brute force when necessary. **11.** Use deception routinely, the Big Lie when necessary. **12.** None of this can show. **13.** This is The System, there shall be no other.

Rule 5 also governs publishing, Editor George. You may remember the era of *Life* and *Look* and *The Saturday Evening Post*. You may have wondered why these mass publications were systematically eliminated and replaced with myriad specialty mags. This was a Rule-5 fragmentation which assured that no longer could everyone be on the same page. Gone was the risk of the wrong editorial choice (an overly vivid war photo for example) triggering some mass disturbance.

Divisions of population is my science, of course, but also divisions deep within the individual. I encourage concepts like the split personality, the bicameral mind, and the bipolar personality. The programming of inner division is my study, the psychology of induced neurosis, inner conflict, psychosis and hallucination.

The Rule-5 ideal is one man alone with a TV, uneasy with himself.

How am I doing?

Rule 6. Control their rhythm and pace.

Industrial orthocracy began with the installation of the town clock, dominating all from its central tower. Before long my clock became indispensable as an intimate personal timepiece as well as a public ubiquity, and my clock remains the primary machine

---

The 13 Rules: 1. Keep them weak. **2.** Keep them dumb. **3.** Keep them scared. **4.** Control all their resources. **5.** Divide and conquer. **6.** Control their rhythm and pace. **7.** Control their chemistry. **8.** Control their sex. **9.** Jack them around. **10.** Use coercion routinely, brute force when necessary. **11.** Use deception routinely, the Big Lie when necessary. **12.** None of this can show. **13.** This is The System, there shall be no other.

of the orthocracy, keeping all subjects marching to the same drum, my drum. My clock liberates the individual from his unregimented bio-rhythms and imposes the reliable, rigorous, predictable rhythms of orthocratic time.

Orthocratic government maintains the official beat with scrupulous precision by means of the Time Register, which is dependably slaved to the rhythm of atomic decay and which continually throbs through the ether on shortwave.

Embraced by orthocratic time, the pace of a population can be adjusted to suit the system – usually in the direction of acceleration. Gone is the siesta. Push them until they are tired; then give them coffee. My accomplishments: the 75-mph freeway, the 200 mph bullet train, and the New York Minute. Keep moving, please. A little faster, please.

Once in control of time, Orthocracy can toy with it a bit, and, in the spirit of Rule 9, institute Daylight Savings Time. As with the clock, so with that ancient allied invention, the calendar, which has been responsibly administered by dominant orthocracies down through the centuries, effectively freeing the individual from the beat of the universe and other interference so that the incessant beat of orthocratic time can rule.

Orthocracy is a pacemaker implanted deep inside, controlling the fundamental throb of life. Be clear,

---

The 13 Rules: 1. Keep them weak. **2.** Keep them dumb, **3.** Keep them scared. **4.** Control all their resources. **5.** Divide and conquer. **6.** Control their rhythm and pace. **7.** Control their chemistry. **8.** Control their sex. **9.** Jack them around. **10.** Use coercion routinely, brute force when necessary. **11.** Use deception routinely, the Big Lie when necessary. **12.** None of this can show. **13.** This is The System, there shall be no other.

readers, as we move into Rule 7, that I am not only a permeating presence but a deeply penetrating one.

I'll say. The penetrating beat of the system and all, Gee, Orthocracy. It sounds almost sexual.

Oh, yes. Consider Rule 8. Your own colloquial honors the sexy, penetrating me with terms like "fucked over" and "mind-fuck" and other derivatives of that root. I take these expressions as flattery.

Continuing then with my penetrating rules ...

Rule 7. Control their chemistry.

It is simply a matter of identifying the various *vectors* of penetration into the body, into the bloodstream, into the psyche, into the soul. There are environmental vectors like air and water, the chemistry of which can be enhanced by industrial vectors, often yielding desirable Rule-1 impacts. The water supply is a great vector. Fluoridation is Rule 7 dancing with Rule 1.

Genetic modification of crops enhances the orthocratic value of the food supply. Industrial vectors can be reinforced by aerial-spraying programs, which can be conducted on a global basis. Thus atmospheric chemistry can be managed and earth-chemistry can be modified, facilitating agricultural management.

The 13 Rules: 1. Keep them weak. **2.** Keep them dumb. **3.** Keep them scared. **4.** Control all their resources. **5.** Divide and conquer. **6.** Control their rhythm and pace. **7.** Control their chemistry. **8.** Control their sex. **9.** Jack them around. **10.** Use coercion routinely, brute force when necessary. **11.** Use deception routinely, the Big Lie when necessary. **12.** None of this can show. **13.** This is The System, there shall be no other.

Such advanced chemical technologies make this a great era for orthocratic development.

Pharmacology is a vector. Pharmaceuticals can deliver chemistries and impacts not necessarily disclosed to the trusting consumer. Certain pharmaceuticals can penetrate the molecular structure of cells and alter functioning. This can also be done by means of vectors that move invisibly through the ether deep into the molecular structure of the living cell. These are the vectors of radiation – electric, microwave, x-ray, and nuclear.

Certain chemistries are orthocratically congenial; others are not. Orthocracy discourages consciousness-expanding shamanistic drugs of the "green" culture, like marijuana and LSD, in the spirit of Rule 2. Conversely, Orthocracy encourages alcohol and other mind-numbing chemicals and also the anodynes and tranquilizers (colloquially "reds"). Orthocracy also promotes the antidepressants ("yellows") like prozac and the acceleration chemicals ("whites") like caffeine, cocaine, and the amphetamines, in the spirit of Rule 6. As an orthocratic dividend, recreational pharmacology creates an urban demographic in which the population divides into subcultures along the above-cited color-lines (Rule 5).

So, evidently, Orthocracy, if everyone shared in the same drug, and in the worst-case scenario, one of those green shaministic drugs, you would not be happy?

The 13 Rules: 1. Keep them weak. **2.** Keep them dumb, **3.** Keep them scared. **4.** Control all their resources. **5.** Divide and conquer. **6.** Control their rhythm and pace. **7.** Control their chemistry. **8.** Control their sex. **9.** Jack them around. **10.** Use coercion routinely, brute force when necessary. **11.** Use deception routinely, the Big Lie when necessary. **12.** None of this can show. **13.** This is The System, there shall be no other.

You describe a regression to the practices of some barbaric pre-orthocratic culture. That's my worst nightmare. Ecstatic thousands in any shared public ritual that isn't baseball. Such a phenomenon would put the whole system at risk.

Sounds a bit like the 1960's, though – Woodstock, the summer of love ...

We're still putting out that fire.

Rule 8. Control their sex.

The managerial impulse of orthocratic rule is flat-out repression of the whole scary phenomenon of sex. So I guess I stand for abstinence. Please appreciate how the aspiring orthocrat so willingly makes that sacrifice and thus honors me at his root. Orthocracy says *No* to procreation. Well, except for a few properly married orthocrats, by artificial insemination, if possible, and the birth by C-section, please. I do promote universal circumcision – any enervation: surgical, chemical, psychic.

Give me the condom, the IUD, the Pill, tied tubes, abortions, vasectomies, cervectomies, mastectomies, and hysterectomies. I will develop each into its own little industry. You might be surprised, however,

The 13 Rules: 1. Keep them weak. **2.** Keep them dumb. **3.** Keep them scared. **4.** Control all their resources. **5.** Divide and conquer. **6.** Control their rhythm and pace. **7.** Control their chemistry. **8.** Control their sex. **9.** Jack them around. **10.** Use coercion routinely, brute force when necessary. **11.** Use deception routinely, the Big Lie when necessary. **12.** None of this can show. **13.** This is The System, there shall be no other.

that I do encourage the industry of pornography. Media is central to Rule 8.

Orthocracy faithfully delivers to the news media the sex criminal of the week, the more famous the criminal, the more sensational. The politician, always a libidinous entity, is no longer exempt from a sex scandal, which gives me a firm hold on him at the root.

Speaking of sex criminals and nonconformists, what about the gays?

Threatening at first, but today the leadership is exhibiting fine orthocratic sensibilities, and the movement is stabilized, at least until the next purge. By the way, it's not called *gay* anymore. Now it is *LGBT*. That identifies four distinct demographics that barely speak to one another (Rule 5). I like the new leadership because it encourages a great domestication, a gentrification unto snobbery, a medicalization unto AIDS, and, of course, a domestication unto matrimony. Appreciate that you might never have heard of that little gay-marriage issue if it had not been pounced upon by the orthocratic media for its great Rule-5 potential.

AIDS: a great orthocratic construct. The gays were great promoters of that Rule-11 adventure and

---

The 13 Rules: 1. Keep them weak. **2.** Keep them dumb, **3.** Keep them scared. **4.** Control all their resources. **5.** Divide and conquer. **6.** Control their rhythm and pace. **7.** Control their chemistry. **8.** Control their sex. **9.** Jack them around. **10.** Use coercion routinely, brute force when necessary. **11.** Use deception routinely, the Big Lie when necessary. **12.** None of this can show. **13.** This is The System, there shall be no other.

helped it to become triumphant. But the fear fades, and Rule 8 craves a new sex pandemic. I have every confidence that the creative orthocrats of medical science will soon come up with another sex-disease novelty, and the gays will promote that one, too, if they are still around.

With fears like AIDS rumbling in the background (Rule 3), I cultivate a world of orthocratic sexiness that delivers a maximum of titillation with a minimum of fulfillment.

I am pleased to report that most climaxes now occur before a video screen.

Sexuality is a wonderful vector for penetrating into the psyche. "First clear the root chakra," said that philosopher of the sex-revolution, Rajneesh, who insisted that such a clearing enabled creative action. No way, I say. Keep those roots tied up in knots.

In the same spirit I apply on special occasions the exquisite disciplines of genital torture. Appreciate, though, that a routine torture can be built into tight underwear. Sex torture, yes. Church rape, prison rape, military rape... These are perennial staples in my Rule-10 toolbox. Sex torture has a desirable way of lingering in the memory – a persistent reminder of my awesome power. Circumcision, performed by a priest of the system at the moment of birth, embeds a lifelong memory and a subconscious respect for me.

The 13 Rules: 1. Keep them weak. **2.** Keep them dumb. **3.** Keep them scared. **4.** Control all their resources. **5.** Divide and conquer. **6.** Control their rhythm and pace. **7.** Control their chemistry. **8.** Control their sex. **9.** Jack them around. **10.** Use coercion routinely, brute force when necessary. **11.** Use deception routinely, the Big Lie when necessary. **12.** None of this can show. **13.** This is The System, there shall be no other.

Rule 9. Jack them around.

No prisoner, soldier, or bureaucrat needs a definition. In police-work, it's the good-cop-bad-cop interrogation. It's conflicting orders to the cornered demonstrators. It's the sting. The joy of exercising the jack-around is the reward of the bureaucrat, who himself is continually jacked around by his superiors.

In orthocratic medicine, Rule 9 is the cure that is always just around the corner but somehow never comes. It's the miracle drug, on which millions have been dependent, suddenly pulled from the shelves as deadly toxic.

Cigarette smoking is one of my greatest Rule-9 accomplishments with a zig-zag history of yes and no all the way through. Today the orthocracy is enjoying the prodigious legislative yield of a Rule-5 ingenuity called second-hand smoke. Any pervasive addiction can be material for a pervasive jack-around.

Jack 'em this way and that way. Jack them up, jack 'em down. A sub-rule: *lift them up before dropping them down.* Ecstatic boom precedes the abysmal bust, a cycle that is standard economics for any properly developed orthocracy. Historically, the intensity of orthocratic rule itself is in a cyclical jack-around of contraction and expansion – one era permissive, the next uptight.

The 13 Rules: 1. Keep them weak. **2.** Keep them dumb, **3.** Keep them scared. **4.** Control all their resources. **5.** Divide and conquer. **6.** Control their rhythm and pace. **7.** Control their chemistry. **8.** Control their sex. **9.** Jack them around. **10.** Use coercion routinely, brute force when necessary. **11.** Use deception routinely, the Big Lie when necessary. **12.** None of this can show. **13.** This is The System, there shall be no other.

Rule 10. Use coercion routinely, brute force when necessary.

This is where the gloves come off and the brass knuckles go on. But please appreciate that into my system are woven coercions more subtle than napalm. Appreciate how the very spirit of force – once established as a social fundamental by violent means – permeates all, and the society drifts naturally into the setting up of situations where coercion is quietly and routinely applied day-to-day through schools, workplaces, banks, churches, families, and so forth, and each of these orthocratic institutions projects a web that binds one coercively to duty and obligation. Ideal is the life where compulsory submission is the dominant theme twenty-four hours a day.

Orthocracy promotes total dependency upon urban infrastructures which can easily be destructed. Everything constructed has a correlative weapon to destruct it. This includes roadways, aqueducts, and electric-power systems. The entire culture of solid-state electronics can be dudded at a stroke by an electromagnetic pulse (EMP) – computers, TV's radios, smart phones. An EMP can shut down the electric-power grid itself. These vulnerabilities are desired.

The 13 Rules: 1. Keep them weak. **2.** Keep them dumb, **3.** Keep them scared. **4.** Control all their resources. **5.** Divide and conquer. **6.** Control their rhythm and pace. **7.** Control their chemistry. **8.** Control their sex. **9.** Jack them around. **10.** Use coercion routinely, brute force when necessary. **11.** Use deception routinely, the Big Lie when necessary. **12.** None of this can show. **13.** This is The System, there shall be no other.

Rule 10 sees to it that any targeted society may have tortuous living conditions inflicted upon it by weapons that tear the infrastructure to pieces: machine guns, artillery, missiles, bombs, including nuclear, yes, but also weapons even more destructive, weapons meteorological and seismic that have the advantage of being totally deniable.

A targeted city, maybe yours, can overnight be turned into a Gaza, a Baghdad, a New Orleans, a Port au Prince. This vulnerability is a fundamental condition of orthocratic existence, and, of course, that condition contributes to a persistent anxiety in the population, a Rule-3 state of mind.

Which brings us to the matter of applying Rule-10 force directly to the human entity in a violent fashion. Appreciate the pathetic vulnerability of this entity which can so easily be coerced in any desired direction by the discrete application of discomfort, pain, and terror. Torture has a million ways, some very exquisite, and Orthocracy knows them all.

Appreciate that all torture does not have to be of the dungeon sort. Little agonies can be built into a society's normal routines. The good orthocrat will cooperate, and he may voluntarily adopt his own agonizing patterns of behavior by which he can torture himself on a daily basis, a religious tribute to me.

Rule 10 is institutionalized in war. War is Orthocracy's highest calling. War is the system in

---

The 13 Rules: 1. Keep them weak. **2.** Keep them dumb, **3.** Keep them scared. **4.** Control all their resources. **5.** Divide and conquer. **6.** Control their rhythm and pace. **7.** Control their chemistry. **8.** Control their sex. **9.** Jack them around. **10.** Use coercion routinely, brute force when necessary. **11.** Use deception routinely, the Big Lie when necessary. **12.** None of this can show. **13.** This is The System, there shall be no other.

celebration. War is the orthocracy in expansion. Perpetual war is desired, perpetual expansion.

A good war can redraw the boundaries of the planet, destroy history, re-plan cities, eliminate surplus real estate and populations, and reinforce orthocratic rule in other respects. War is how I get my way.

My USA has a particular affinity to the institutions of war.

Every geographic sector under orthocratic control has its designated function in the global orthocracy, and Sector USA is the designated war-making platform. This is USA's reward for demonstrating military excellence from the get-go with its aborigines, with it's innovative Civil War, and with its WW2 industrialization.

War is not about winners and losers, the standard narrative notwithstanding, but about sustaining war itself. A war sustained is a war won. Perpetual war is ideal, but, unfortunately, the system cannot run in high gear forever. Rule 12 particularly becomes stressed. There can be embarrassing disclosures. Sustaining war in particular and orthocracy in general greatly depends upon the successful exercise of our next two rules.

The 13 Rules: 1. Keep them weak. **2.** Keep them dumb. **3.** Keep them scared. **4.** Control all their resources. **5.** Divide and conquer. **6.** Control their rhythm and pace. **7.** Control their chemistry. **8.** Control their sex. **9.** Jack them around. **10.** Use coercion routinely, brute force when necessary. **11.** Use deception routinely, the Big Lie when necessary. **12.** None of this can show. **13.** This is The System, there shall be no other.

Rule 11. Use deception routinely, The Big Lie when necessary.

Fortuitous it is that the USA, the designated platform for war-making, is also the designated platform for the production and export of fantasy and inebriation. Appreciate that it is not an easy matter to launch a war against the inevitable public disinclination. Some extreme drama, a Pearl Harbor or a 911, must be successfully contrived, at great effort. Moreover, the associated fictions and psychologies must be vigilantly maintained against exposure, doubt, and fatigue. It is a wearying day-to-day challenge to sustain a war's credibility. It is a task that tires me out and consumes many good generals, publicists, and news anchors.

In accordance with Rule 11, war is narrated as a football game with winners and losers, but the real winner is always me.

Rule 11, particularly in respect to the Big-Lie aspect, is based on Orthocracy's deep faith in human gullibility, a faith that is rarely disappointed. Orthocracy is a student of the science of knowing and of depth-psychology. The industries of Rule 11 are public relations, advertising, entertainment, education, religion, and mass media, the industries of knowledge-management (Rule 2).

One also might factor in for Rule 11 the industries of mood-management like the psycho-pharmaceutical

---

The 13 Rules: 1. Keep them weak. **2.** Keep them dumb. **3.** Keep them scared. **4.** Control all their resources. **5.** Divide and conquer. **6.** Control their rhythm and pace. **7.** Control their chemistry. **8.** Control their sex. **9.** Jack them around. **10.** Use coercion routinely, brute force when necessary. **11.** Use deception routinely, the Big Lie when necessary. **12.** None of this can show. **13.** This is The System, there shall be no other.

and liquor industries, which offer products and promote lifestyles conducive to mental receptivity and programming. Think six-pack, Prozac, the couch-potato and his TV. On comes the evening news. The big story of the day may never have happened and be solely the creation of some Madison Avenue PR firm, a credible source for the media. The viewer's critical faculties, however, have been numbed (Rule 2 again).

Spin and selective editing of the news is broadly suspected, but under-appreciated are my pro-active campaigns of the Big Lie, in which the story generated by the credible source is printed and broadcast repetitively to millions by various centralized coordinated mass media (including entertainment and religious media), all supported by advertising, itself a medium. Thus the creative Big-Lie story becomes a pervasive orthocratic truth eventually to be written as history and propagated by my educators.

Even the media that calls itself "alternative" dare not contradict certain sacred Big-Lie propagandas like AIDS, 911, and global warming, lest they lose their funding from prestigious orthocratic foundations.

Story by story, an environment of orthocratic truth, a pseudo-environment, is synthesized. Thus a mind-world is created consisting of a web of orthocratically congenial delusions which any good orthocrat should be happy to inhabit.

The 13 Rules: 1. Keep them weak. **2.** Keep them dumb, **3.** Keep them scared. **4.** Control all their resources. **5.** Divide and conquer. **6.** Control their rhythm and pace. **7.** Control their chemistry. **8.** Control their sex. **9.** Jack them around. **10.** Use coercion routinely, brute force when necessary. **11.** Use deception routinely, the Big Lie when necessary. **12.** None of this can show. **13.** This is The System, there shall be no other.

The mind-world of Rule-11 truth may be consistent only within itself, may be counter-intuitive to some on its surface, and may even contradict empirical evidence right before their eyes. In this situation, doubt may form and crystallize into skeptical expression and even into action.

A more likely result, however, is a subconscious division and inner conflict in which a superficial belief in the Big Lie is dogged by doubt way down deep. This is a neurotic condition congenial to Rule 5. That same rule also benefits from any real-world conflicts that may arise between those who believe the official truth and those who do not.

As we reach the end of this chapter, let us pause to appreciate how nicely the Rules of Rule work together and applaud the elegant synergy of my beautiful System.

You might also boast, Orthocracy, that when we finish this chapter you will have parsed all 13 rules of rule in just 25 pages. Any respectable academic would have taken at least 300. Your editor appreciates your efficiency.

Plenty of words for me. I am getting tired.

The 13 Rules: 1. Keep them weak. **2.** Keep them dumb, **3.** Keep them scared. **4.** Control all their resources. **5.** Divide and conquer. **6.** Control their rhythm and pace. **7.** Control their chemistry. **8.** Control their sex. **9.** Jack them around. **10.** Use coercion routinely, brute force when necessary. **11.** Use deception routinely, the Big Lie when necessary. **12.** None of this can show. **13.** This is The System, there shall be no other.

Rule 12. None of this can show.

All knowledge relating to, or even faintly suggestive, of the inner workings of my system must be occluded from the public eye. However, for my system to function, there must be some who know more than the rabble, but this knowledge must be compartmentalized and classified and made accessible only to an orthocratic elite of the investigated and cleared.

If Rule 11 were one-hundred-percent effective (and it is getting there), *none* of this would show, because it would be completely covered up by deceptions. Please, no revelations to disturb my world. No surprises.

It is important for the orthocrat, especially if he goes before the public, to master the Rule-12 skill of immobilizing the upper lip, lest it quiver out some tell-tale message from the unconscious.

There are many leaks in the system, and its workings sometimes can be divined by smart observation and by intelligent deduction (due to a failure of Rule 2). There may arise on occasion instances of doubt and skepticism about events as presented, leading to the excavation of unpleasant facts and the threat of exposure, confrontation, and embarrassment. Any action that could conceivably result from such revelations must be choreographed into predictable rituals by my dissidence managers.

The 13 Rules: 1. Keep them weak. **2.** Keep them dumb. **3.** Keep them scared. **4.** Control all their resources. **5.** Divide and conquer. **6.** Control their rhythm and pace. **7.** Control their chemistry. **8.** Control their sex. **9.** Jack them around. **10.** Use coercion routinely, brute force when necessary. **11.** Use deception routinely, the Big Lie when necessary. **12.** None of this can show. **13.** This is The System, there shall be no other.

Dissidence managers? That is an interesting concept, Orthocracy. Please explain.

Surprisingly, not everyone loves my system. Dissidence arises and must be managed. For example, some of my more sensitive subjects, because their morality and sensibility is inadequately adjusted, may be uncomfortable with orthocratic rule and determined to dis-identify themselves with my nasty system. You might call this group the good-people demographic. For them my dissidence-management industry has created a refreshing new identity and lifestyle that resides comfortably in the groves of academe, in so-called alternative media, in organized peace-and-justice activism, and in the great orthocratic foundations that quietly pay the bills.

For the good-people demographic, cable TV produces daily rituals of sophisticated political satire. The Internet and alternative radio compile daily inventories of the crimes of my greedy capitalists, accompanied by the appropriate lamentations, ideology, and utopianism. Alternative media has proven to be a reliable vector for propagating orthocratic science, including such Rule-11 adventures as AIDS, 911, and global warming. By such management, the energy of dissidence is diverted into harmless rituals. Then, instead of action, there is only activism. Dissidence-management is an important orthocratic industry, and none of its bones can show.

The 13 Rules: 1. Keep them weak. **2.** Keep them dumb, **3.** Keep them scared. **4.** Control all their resources. **5.** Divide and conquer. **6.** Control their rhythm and pace. **7.** Control their chemistry. **8.** Control their sex. **9.** Jack them around. **10.** Use coercion routinely, brute force when necessary. **11.** Use deception routinely, the Big Lie when necessary. **12.** None of this can show. **13.** This is The System, there shall be no other.

Rule 13. This is The System; there shall be no other.

The orthocracy is never wrong. It can only admit to the occasional mistake. Orthocracy is the only system, and it must roll like an armored tank over any deviant culture on the planet. Orthocracy must prevail universally to the exclusion of all other social forms. Orthocracy is a fragile idea and cannot stand much competition. That an aboriginal tribal culture or two may still be lingering stubbornly in some obscure territory on the planet is an abhorrence, a threat, and a challenge to all orthocracies on the planet, and one orthocracy or another, on one pretext or another, will rise up, meet the challenge, and eradicate the deviant.

A deviant culture may inspire some subculture to arise spontaneously from within an established orthocracy, and that subculture is a threat requiring attention before it spreads.

Orthocracy thrives when any other ruling system is unimaginable. Orthocratic education is conducted accordingly. Scrupulously excluded from the curriculum is any hint that something like a ruling system may even exist (Rule 2 abetting Rule 13).

What about all those ideals of democracy, especially in my USA, the founding fathers and all?

The 13 Rules: 1. Keep them weak. **2.** Keep them dumb, **3.** Keep them scared. **4.** Control all their resources. **5.** Divide and conquer. **6.** Control their rhythm and pace. **7.** Control their chemistry. **8.** Control their sex. **9.** Jack them around. **10.** Use coercion routinely, brute force when necessary. **11.** Use deception routinely, the Big Lie when necessary. **12.** None of this can show. **13.** This is The System, there shall be no other.

Democracy is a Rule-11 artifact. Your founding fathers were good European orthocrats.

You may conduct a democratic election in the name of "change," but you will always end up with same-old-me. You may conduct a violent revolution and overthrow this or that orthocratic government, but you always end up with me. That is because, in accordance with Rule 13, you really do know no other.

Rule 13 dictates continual expansion of the orthocracy. This is the Rule-13 imperative. The universal fulfillment of Rule 13 is orthocracy's highest purpose. A campaign in the name of Rule 13 always has the highest priority, and flowing to the cause is limitless funding (and blood). You may wonder why growth is the obsession of all government, industry, and religion and why development is God. The answer is Rule 13.

Orthocracy is mass rule, and so Orthocracy resents any tribal form of social organization. Loyalty must be directed into transcendent orthocratic institutions. Orthocracy resents extended families, especially under the same roof. Orthocracy resents any society that is communal, cooperative, or communistic (Rule 5). Orthocracy resents subsistence agriculture (Rule 4). Orthocracy resents shaman-ism (Rule 2). All societies lingering on the primitive model must ultimately succumb to orthocratic rule, says Rule 13.

The 13 Rules: 1. Keep them weak. **2.** Keep them dumb, **3.** Keep them scared. **4.** Control all their resources. **5.** Divide and conquer. **6.** Control their rhythm and pace. **7.** Control their chemistry. **8.** Control their sex. **9.** Jack them around. **10.** Use coercion routinely, brute force when necessary. **11.** Use deception routinely, the Big Lie when necessary. **12.** None of this can show. **13.** This is The System, there shall be no other.

In this effort, the violence of the Rule-10 arsenal need not always be applied. Orthocracy can be insinuated peacefully by means of missionaries, Hiltons, global-bank loans, and by one or another industrial process that conducts the population into the rigors of the 60-hour workweek.

Of course, if these options fail, Rule 10 clicks in, and there is war. Most war is conducted in the name of Rule 13.

A deviant society may have survived because it is located in some inaccessible topology, the penetration of which is a challenge to weapons technology. The attack helicopter was progress, and now robotic aerial-attack vehicles are among the weapons available to open up these obscure regions to proper orthocratic development. In the extreme, a recalcitrant society may have to be softened by some dramatic, terrifying, and hugely destructive event, like a good nuking.

I am a jealous god, and when I don't get my way, I will opt for scorched earth.

The 13 Rules: 1. Keep them weak. **2.** Keep them dumb. **3.** Keep them scared. **4.** Control all their resources. **5.** Divide and conquer. **6.** Control their rhythm and pace. **7.** Control their chemistry. **8.** Control their sex. **9.** Jack them around. **10.** Use coercion routinely, brute force when necessary. **11.** Use deception routinely, the Big Lie when necessary. **12.** None of this can show. **13.** This is The System, there shall be no other.

Part Three:
Orthocracy Speaks on the Issues of the Day

"Issues" you are asking for, Editor George? I do encourage the very idea of "issues." Issues feed Rule 5. They are junk food for the political mind (Rule 2). Above all, "the issues of the day" assure that day-to-day I am never seen whole (Rule 12). When issue-consciousness prevails, each of my so-called "crimes" can become its own independent issue with its own coterie of followers and fund-raising apparatus.

Issues feed my dissidence-management industry, generating endless discussions, orations, analyses, papers, books, articles, blogs, websites, workshops, thinktanks, broadcasts, conferences, grants, rallies, demonstrations, occupations, boycotts, ballots, bullets, and other distracting rituals that drain energy from the body politic.

I say "yes" to issues. I will even invent an issue now and then and launch it unexpectedly into a surprised and disarmed body politic. For example, no big issue exists, and then some astute orthocrat – preacher, politician, journalist – perceives the hot-button of righteousness and how the interests of the orthocracy and his own ambitions can be served by pumping that button into a burning issue between opposing parties. Then all it takes is my mass media jumping upon it, and suddenly you have the abortion issue, the gay-marriage issue. Whatever the issue, it will not focus on me, and it will roll to my benefit.

The 13 Rules: 1. Keep them weak. **2.** Keep them dumb, **3.** Keep them scared. **4.** Control all their resources. **5.** Divide and conquer. **6.** Control their rhythm and pace. **7.** Control their chemistry. **8.** Control their sex. **9.** Jack them around. **10.** Use coercion routinely, brute force when necessary. **11.** Use deception routinely, the Big Lie when necessary. **12.** None of this can show. **13.** This is The System, there shall be no other.

I speak here of the energy of Rule 5, the energy of polarity, that universal force between the magnetic poles, between electric plus and minus, between yin and yang. Politics has its own electric physics, and it is my business to establish opposing poles and to manipulate the resulting human-energy resource (Rule 4).

Each to his own pet issue, I say, this one today, that one tomorrow. May a smörgåsbord of urgent issues engage the energies of all good citizens who hunger to exercise their indignation on something, on anything. Orthocracy promotes single-issue activism, multi-issue dilettantism, and everybody-for-nothing.

Everybody for nothing?

Like Hands Across America, The Walk for AIDS, The Race for the Cure, The Million-man March, Earth Day, the Obama election … you get the idea. I speak of the orthocratic solidarity of everybody-for-nothing.

What about a march for peace?

If war is the orthocracy in high gear, then what can a demonstration for peace mean? It means another single-issue distraction, assuring that I shall never be seen whole. Everybody for nothing.

The 13 Rules: 1. Keep them weak. **2.** Keep them dumb, **3.** Keep them scared. **4.** Control all their resources. **5.** Divide and conquer. **6.** Control their rhythm and pace. **7.** Control their chemistry. **8.** Control their sex. **9.** Jack them around. **10.** Use coercion routinely, brute force when necessary. **11.** Use deception routinely, the Big Lie when necessary. **12.** None of this can show. **13.** This is The System, there shall be no other.

And the current Occupy movement?

I am the occupation. And this little movement: it will be everybody for nothing, if I have anything to do with it. My dissidence-management teams are crawling all over this movement.

The protesters do seem a bit uncertain about what they are protesting. I guess this vagueness makes them vulnerable. Frankly, Orthocracy, I think in their hearts they are protesting You. So many say, "well, it's all fucked," and I think the "all" in that sentence is You.

I am flattered.

Anyway, the Occupy march gets underway, and some journalist asks why, and they feel compelled to explain themselves and to sanctify some particular issue, any issue, as a platform, and everybody has to get on board, and they come up with a slogan, "We are the 99 percent," which means that a tiny one-percent elite has all of the money and power.

You are seeing here the work of my dissidence managers. It is their job to manage the clichés. About slogans in general: it is important to maintain political consciousness at the word-deep level (Rule

---

The 13 Rules: 1. Keep them weak. **2.** Keep them dumb. **3.** Keep them scared. **4.** Control all their resources. **5.** Divide and conquer. **6.** Control their rhythm and pace. **7.** Control their chemistry. **8.** Control their sex. **9.** Jack them around. **10.** Use coercion routinely, brute force when necessary. **11.** Use deception routinely, the Big Lie when necessary. **12.** None of this can show. **13.** This is The Systom, there shall be no other.

2). Word-deep opens portals to neuro-linguistic programming. Word-deep consciousness can be manipulated by savvy word-craft (Rule 11), and I have plenty of savvy word-crafters in my employ.

Word-deep consciousness is congenial to a Christian biblical culture that stresses the authority of The Word. Such a culture flourishes in your USA, George.

I like clichés. I like that 99 percent slogan. It reinforces the old left cliché of economic determinism, which says the ruling system resides in an elite of greedy, fat, cigar-smoking white men – a concept that feeds class-conflict (Rule 5). This consciousness assures that I shall forever remain invisible (Rule 12).

Are you saying that your system is not a top-down affair?

Not really. My system is authoritarian, and it is autocratic. But my system is not installed in an elite. Rather the elite is installed in my system. It is, however, important to maintain the old left mythology. Apparently, my dissidence managers are on the case with this Occupy movement.

Do you mean that paid agents of the government are infiltrating the Occupy movement?

The 13 Rules: 1. Keep them weak. **2.** Keep them dumb, **3.** Keep them scared. **4.** Control all their resources. **5.** Divide and conquer. **6.** Control their rhythm and pace. **7.** Control their chemistry. **8.** Control their sex. **9.** Jack them around. **10.** Use coercion routinely, brute force when necessary. **11.** Use deception routinely, the Big Lie when necessary. **12.** None of this can show. **13.** This is The System, there shall be no other.

Some of that, of course. But it is more a matter of an established consciousness, a consciousness resigned and reasonable, a gentrified consciousness. There is a progressive gentry that moves right in with its own little occupation wherever political novelty is sensed. Any new movement will want to absorb some of the gentry's respectability, credibility, academic standing, and media access.

The liberal gentry knows in its orthocratic bones just what to do. It feeds upon spontaneous political energy like a vampire. It manages the clichés. It engages the movement in endless academic discussions. It marches the movement around the city, here and there, on this issue, that issue. Yes, the gentry will gentrify the movement, and it will bleed it.

I don't know, Orthocracy, these protesters do march with a particular spirit and resolve, and the protest has achieved an impressive magnitude and intensity, don't you think? Some say the genie is out of the bottle and that it cannot be put back. But you remain unperturbed. Correct?

Unperturbed? Not really, I must admit that manifested here is the spirit that worries me most. To any true orthocrat, the spirit of anarchy set in motion is a scary thing, and in this movement there is, as you say, a particular magnitude and intensity.

The 13 Rules: 1. Keep them weak. **2.** Keep them dumb, **3.** Keep them scared. **4.** Control all their resources. **5.** Divide and conquer. **6.** Control their rhythm and pace. **7.** Control their chemistry. **8.** Control their sex. **9.** Jack them around. **10.** Use coercion routinely, brute force when necessary. **11.** Use deception routinely, the Big Lie when necessary. **12.** None of this can show. **13.** This is The System, there shall be no other.

In these occupation encampments, the convening itself is a threat and represents a serious melt-down of Rule 5. And there is a lot of screwing around (Rule-8 violations), I understand.

Appreciate that the modern urban orthocracy is planned for a minimum of public space for any convening. In the USA planning is particularly progressive in this respect. The proper public space is the high-security shopping mall with a 9:00 PM curfew. The new city park is designed on security criteria to facilitate surveillance and no-place-to-hide. The occupiers will be harassed by government on one legal pretext or another, but it is the Rule-5 violations in such encampments that are the real concern.

I don't mean to alarm you, Orthocracy, but I think Rule 5 may be more fragile than you imagine. For example, in New York City, where your Rule-5 rules as nowhere else, all you need is a blackout or a snowstorm. Suddenly all the normal structures of alienation crumble. People talk with their neighbors in the hallways and streets.

The same thing happens after a good bombing.

Also, in the New York snowstorm or blackout, there is a great slow-down, in violation of Rule 6 and of the New York minute. Traffic stops, and a great quiet descends, relieving the noise-induced anxiety. Then people begin to

---

The 13 Rules: 1. Keep them weak. **2.** Keep them dumb, **3.** Keep them scared. **4.** Control all their resources. **5.** Divide and conquer. **6.** Control their rhythm and pace. **7.** Control their chemistry. **8.** Control their sex. **9.** Jack them around. **10.** Use coercion routinely, brute force when necessary. **11.** Use deception routinely, the Big Lie when necessary. **12.** None of this can show. **13.** This is The System, there shall be no other.

work out shared problems cooperatively in violation of Rule 5. The system begins to melt.

It is important for this reason to get government responders on the scene as soon as possible.

In an encampment situation, Rule 5 dissolves, as you admit, and along with it Rule 6 and Rule 8, as you have observed, and couldn't this continue to the ultimate emergency, a breakdown of Rule 13?

That is why these encampments must be firmly Rule-10-ed. I admit it. All this convening and activism everywhere is scary. However, in such a crisis Orthocracy tries to take the long historical view and stay cool. The situation has been seen before, and, if it continues, the usual corrective will be applied.

By which you mean, I ask with some dread?

OK, a little war may be necessary. Maybe even a big one.

Another war. Oh dear.
But we have been digressing, Orthocracy, and it is time we moved this chapter on to the issues of the day, as we have promised. However, this presents a problem of

---

The 13 Rules: 1. Keep them weak. **2.** Keep them dumb. **3.** Keep them scared. **4.** Control all their resources. **5.** Divide and conquer. **6.** Control their rhythm and pace. **7.** Control their chemistry. **8.** Control their sex. **9.** Jack them around. **10.** Use coercion routinely, brute force when necessary. **11.** Use deception routinely, the Big Lie when necessary. **12.** None of this can show. **13.** This is The System, there shall be no other.

editorial selection, because, as you say, the issues are so abundant. So allow me to choose some issues of substance and to limit the count to an arbitrary, well, thirteen, and I shall select these issues from a perusal of the news headlines circa summer-fall, 2011 beginning with:

1. Afghanistan

Afghanistan is back in the news with more talk of a troop draw-down. Also there is an appreciation of the tenth anniversary of the USA's longest war.

Afghanistan is a good place to start, George. Any place where my bombs are exploding is sure to qualify as an issue of substance. Afghanistan I celebrate. A war sustained is a war won. Pundits like to say that the war is being lost. This is nonsense. The sustaining is the winning. But, with any war, Rule 12 does get strained over time, hence the talk of troop draw-downs. If this does occur, the project will continue on a covert level.

Afghanistan is the classic Rule-13 war. Afghanistan is an on-going responsibility undertaken dutifully from time to time by one or another of the major orthocracies: UK, USSR, USA… Regardless of the nation, citizens of the warring orthocracy of the day scratch their heads and wonder, "Why are we in Afghanistan? Such an expenditure of

---

The 13 Rules: 1. Keep them weak. **2.** Keep them dumb, **3.** Keep them scared. **4.** Control all their resources. **5.** Divide and conquer. **6.** Control their rhythm and pace. **7.** Control their chemistry. **8.** Control their sex. **9.** Jack them around. **10.** Use coercion routinely, brute force when necessary. **11.** Use deception routinely, the Big Lie when necessary. **12.** None of this can show. **13.** This is The System, there shall be no other.

resources and blood! How can this be justified? Such a pointless war?"

They do not know the Rule-13 imperative. To expand orthocratic rule is the supreme priority of orthocratic rule. The more developed any particular national orthocracy the more responsible that nation must be to the Rule-13 imperative, especially if the orthocracy happens to be the designated wehrmacht platform for the globe, like your USA, George.

Good citizens of the wehrmacht state do not know about the Rule-13 imperative, and they should not know (Rule 12). So tell them it's Bin Laden.

And now that your Bin Laden is so dramatically gone?

It was time to bring the aging 911 narrative full circle to a proper resolution. TV-watchers are accustomed to the resolved narrative with no loose strings. Bin Laden's going clears the way for the next generation of crisis myth. Look out for that.

Bin Laden "dramatically" gone, you say. Yes dramatic indeed, quite a piece of theater, don't you think? I celebrate the Bin-Laden execution as a successful performance, as I celebrate that entire piece of theater called *911*. The more implausible the story, the greater my satisfaction when it does go down (Rule 11).

The 13 Rules: 1. Keep them weak. **2.** Keep them dumb. **3.** Keep them scared. **4.** Control all their resources. **5.** Divide and conquer. **6.** Control their rhythm and pace. **7.** Control their chemistry. **8.** Control their sex. **9.** Jack them around. **10.** Use coercion routinely, brute force when necessary. **11.** Use deception routinely, the Big Lie when necessary. **12.** None of this can show. **13.** This is The System, there shall be no other.

Appreciate that each venture in myth-making is a bit experimental. "Run it up the flagpole and see if they salute it," we say. But will they? It is an experiment every time. I do get nervous. Things can go wrong.

"Theater? Performance?" Are you saying that the Bin Laden assassination was staged?

Not even staged. Just announced, and the details filled in later. Actually, Bin Laden is alive and well on a ranch in Crawford, Texas. I share these little secrets with you, George.

I shall not tell a soul.

But the subject here is Afghanistan. That territory is a perennial mess, a violation of all good orthocratic sensibilities: backward tribal cultures tenaciously holding out in inaccessible terrain, unanswerable to any central government. Religious extremism. Anarchy! Weirdly dressed cultures with outrageous sex customs in defiance of Rule-8 standards. Slow and lazy in defiance of Rule 6. Fortunately, technologies are becoming available that can deal more effectively with these resistants, robotic aircraft for example.

The 13 Rules: 1. Keep them weak. **2.** Keep them dumb, **3.** Keep them scared. **4.** Control all their resources. **5.** Divide and conquer. **6.** Control their rhythm and pace. **7.** Control their chemistry. **8.** Control their sex. **9.** Jack them around. **10.** Use coercion routinely, brute force when necessary. **11.** Use deception routinely, the Big Lie when necessary. **12.** None of this can show. **13.** This is The System, there shall be no other.

Those tenacious cultures seem to have survived invasion and occupation by three major orthocracies.

And the project may eventually require a fourth. Afghanistan is not an easy road. But I see a happier day in the utopian future when the surviving minority population of the old deviant cultures, having been pacified in refugee camps, will labor peacefully on agribiz plantations producing a new genetically-modified poppy. Other survivors will be inducted into service work in the humming metropolis of New Kabul, a tourist destination with a Las Vegas flavor.

Come on, Orthocracy, Kabul a tourist destination?

As a matter of fact, a Kabul Marriot rises as we speak. Appreciate also that, amidst the apparent chaos, a couple of TV networks have been constructed, allowing the free flow of information to the Afghans from professional orthocratic producers. This is progress.

And the future?

The 13 Rules: 1. Keep them weak. **2.** Keep them dumb. **3.** Keep them scared. **4.** Control all their resources. **5.** Divide and conquer. **6.** Control their rhythm and pace. **7.** Control their chemistry. **8.** Control their sex. **9.** Jack them around. **10.** Use coercion routinely, brute force when necessary. **11.** Use deception routinely, the Big Lie when necessary. **12.** None of this can show. **13.** This is The System, there shall be no other.

The emerging Afghan orthocracy will expand to embrace a pacified Pakistan and India, and all three will merge at last into a centrally administered orthocratic union. Now, does that sound like a pointless war? Good orthocrats must keep the faith and maintain a firm vision of the future, no matter what.

2. Guantanamo

The USA's off-shore prison is in the news because the President has promised its closure, and people are wondering, when?

Guantanamo was an important prop for a scene or two in that major theatrical production called *911*. If you declare a terrorist attack, you need some terrorists to show.

By now Guantanamo has lost its utility and has become a bit of an inconvenience. However, it is unlikely to go away any time soon, having been firmly planted as a fixture in the post-911 orthocracy.

The prison debuted as the outdoor Camp X-ray, and, through the fences, the caged terrorist specimens got televised for the world. That some of these terrorists were just street vendors or cab drivers does not matter. When terrorists are needed for the cast, terrorists will be found. The show must go on.

The 13 Rules: 1. Keep them weak. **2.** Keep them dumb. **3.** Keep them scared. **4.** Control all their resources. **5.** Divide and conquer. **6.** Control their rhythm and pace. **7.** Control their chemistry. **8.** Control their sex. **9.** Jack them around. **10.** Use coercion routinely, brute force when necessary. **11.** Use deception routinely, the Big Lie when necessary. **12.** None of this can show. **13.** This is The System, there shall be no other.

The Camp X-ray prisoners soon disappeared behind prison walls to emerge later in ominous news stories. The terrorists are allowed no lawyers, no rights. They regularly suffer torture and abuse. They may be held forever. Thus Guantanamo, the production, defined the new Rule-10 parameters for the post-911 era.

"Guantanamo the production." I hadn't realized, Orthocracy, that you are so much the man of show biz. Gives you a bit of glamor, I mean.

As I am all about Rule 11, so I am all about show biz.

As a matter of fact, the producer-genius in me visualizes a major stage production. Remember *Stalag 17*? Coming soon to Broadway: "Guantanamo, The Musical-Comedy." What do you think?

3. Solitary Confinement

In the news because prisoners are hunger-striking on the issue at Pelican Bay and elsewhere. Is solitary confinement torture? Overcrowding is also in the news. The high court of California has ruled the release of 30,000 hard-won prisoners until finances can be found to build more facilities.

The 13 Rules: 1. Keep them weak. **2.** Keep them dumb. **3.** Keep them scared. **4.** Control all their resources. **5.** Divide and conquer. **6.** Control their rhythm and pace. **7.** Control their chemistry. **8.** Control their sex. **9.** Jack them around. **10.** Use coercion routinely, brute force when necessary. **11.** Use deception routinely, the Big Lie when necessary. **12.** None of this can show. **13.** This is The System, there shall be no other.

Is solitary torture? OK, I admit it. So why this rigorous practice, and why this continuous expansion of prison facilities and population?

Please understand the fundamental here. Prison is the orthocracy fulfilled. Examine the rules of rule, and you will see what I mean. For example, Rule 1. Imprisonment is disablement. Solitary confinement is certainly a fulfillment of Rule 5, and in sensory deprivation, Rule 2 also finds fulfillment. The punitive spirit of Rule 10 is fulfilled in imprisonment, in solitary, and in the routine tortures of prison existence. Rule 13 promotes the continuous expansion of this central and iconic orthocratic institution.

Prison, like war, is a realization of the orthocratic apotheosis. Prison is the system fulfilled in a single institution. As long as you have my orthocracy, so will you have prisons, and more and more of them. Prison-building is irresistible to the orthocracy.

Orthocracy, you seem to be saying that a population held in imprisonment and continuous war would be the ideal orthocratic society. Correct?

Orthocracy's wet dream is a Gaza.

In orthocracies more typical, such as your USA, George, there are the innumerable prisoners behind bars, yes, but the prison orthocracy expands in widening circles to embrace the electronically

---

The 13 Rules: 1. Keep them weak. **2.** Keep them dumb, **3.** Keep them scared. **4.** Control all their resources. **5.** Divide and conquer. **6.** Control their rhythm and pace. **7.** Control their chemistry. **8.** Control their sex. **9.** Jack them around. **10.** Use coercion routinely, brute force when necessary. **11.** Use deception routinely, the Big Lie when necessary. **12.** None of this can show. **13.** This is The System, there shall be no other.

monitored, the house-arrested, the parolee, and the probationer. Then you must count other populations under detention: the illegal immigrant, the terrorist suspect, the secretly held. You could also factor in a vast encamped refugee population of displaced millions.

Also, under certain crisis circumstances, it may be necessary to detain huge segments of the general population as vaguely suspect, and facilities exist out in the countryside, under Rule-12 cover, to imprison them. Every major city must have its own sports stadium capable of imprisoning tens of thousands, and it must be a new stadium of the appropriate scale, and the architecture must otherwise anticipate the detention contingency. Thanks to generous public funding, this urban mandate has been largely fulfilled, especially in your USA, George.

Gee, my progressive USA.

Also, George, your USA is the world leader in prison technology and design. The solitary-confinement model is the invention of good Quaker orthocrats way back in your nation's history. In the initial Philadelphia model, all prisoners were held in solitary. Hallways radiated in spokes from a central core of control, an architecture honored today in the layout of a supermax facility, such as Pelican Bay. Sensory deprivation was

---

The 13 Rules: 1. Keep them weak. **2.** Keep them dumb. **3.** Keep them scared. **4.** Control all their resources. **5.** Divide and conquer. **6.** Control their rhythm and pace. **7.** Control their chemistry. **8.** Control their sex. **9.** Jack them around. **10.** Use coercion routinely, brute force when necessary. **11.** Use deception routinely, the Big Lie when necessary. **12.** None of this can show. **13.** This is The System, there shall be no other.

in that original Quaker model. Guards padded around noiselessly on soft slippers.

George, your USA is also the current per-capita world leader in the recruitment of prison population, and your USA will soon be competitive with China in prison industrial production. Inevitably, the largest prison populations reside in the most highly developed orthocracies.

Orthocracy, if prison is the system institutionalized, then isn't orthocratic society at large a sort of prison? I asked an architect friend, who was ascending rapidly in government bureaucracies charged with public-housing, what is your background? He said,"prison design."

Yes, my system is astute at building informal little prisons everywhere. Some are architectural. Appreciate generally that the architecture of civilization is an orthocratic construct. Also some of my prisons are immaterial, being constructed in the mind.

4. Iraq

Continuing with issues where the bombings are, Iraq is also in the news with talk of a troop draw-down.

The 13 Rules: 1. Keep them weak. **2.** Keep them dumb, **3.** Keep them scared. **4.** Control all their resources. **5.** Divide and conquer. **6.** Control their rhythm and pace. **7.** Control their chemistry. **8.** Control their sex. **9.** Jack them around. **10.** Use coercion routinely, brute force when necessary. **11.** Use deception routinely, the Big Lie when necessary. **12.** None of this can show. **13.** This is The System, there shall be no other.

The Iraq war is another prize-winner for duration like Afghanistan. Yes, the sustaining is the winning. A continuing military presence in itself is a healthy orthocratic influence upon a culture, regardless of whatever win-lose vicissitudes are recorded in the official military history. My very presence assures some "nation-building."

Nation-building, in quotes?

That is a euphemism. When you are nation-building, you are building me.

Iraq is a Rule-1 war. A threat to the global orthocracy is any nation that becomes too independent and strong. Rule 1 implies a multinational balance of powerlessness. We also have here another Rule-13 war, a candidate for which is any nation nonconforming with the evolving global orthocracy in any way, or any nation demonstrating any potential or any inclination to nonconform in any way. Everybody please align with Orthocracy's plans for the future global order – or else. This is the tacit message of Iraq. It may be necessary to repeat it elsewhere.

But all the pundits call the Iraq war a failure.

The 13 Rules: 1. Keep them weak. **2.** Keep them dumb. **3.** Keep them scared. **4.** Control all their resources. **5.** Divide and conquer. **6.** Control their rhythm and pace. **7.** Control their chemistry. **8.** Control their sex. **9.** Jack them around. **10.** Use coercion routinely, brute force when necessary. **11.** Use deception routinely, the Big Lie when necessary. **12.** None of this can show. **13.** This is The System, there shall be no other.

It must be declared a "failure" for reasons of Rules 11 and 12, but the Iraq war is in fact a great success. It has successfully reduced a once overly functional society to a more desirable level of dysfunction and disarray (Rule 1). Citizens of the educated middle-class, always a threat (Rule 2), are gone, along with a few million other inconvenient entities. Bombs explode, chaos rules, and that is my opportunity to edit the population, to make other social reforms, and to do some nation-building.

Speaking of bombing, in Iraq we see the substitution of the traditional aerial type, which has obvious Rule-12 deficiencies, with what you might call *ground bombing*. Random explosions of obscure origin (covertly arranged, often robotic) surprise the public as it tries to go about its daily business. This guerrilla-style asymmetrical warfare is Rule 9 applied at the extreme. By such means, any society can be unnerved and worn down over time, so that eventually the people are begging for order, my order.

The Iraq war is developing the template for prolonged low-intensity warfare, exportable to anywhere on the planet, including the USA itself.

My USA, the wehrmacht platform itself, is not exempt?

There is still much work to be done on Orthocracy USA.

The 13 Rules: 1. Keep them weak. **2.** Keep them dumb, **3.** Keep them scared. **4.** Control all their resources. **5.** Divide and conquer. **6.** Control their rhythm and pace. **7.** Control their chemistry. **8.** Control their sex. **9.** Jack them around. **10.** Use coercion routinely, brute force when necessary. **11.** Use deception routinely, the Big Lie when necessary. **12.** None of this can show. **13.** This is The System, there shall be no other.

Appreciate that the Iraq and Afghan wars also function as on-the-job training platforms for a new generation of warrior personnel. Appreciate that when you kill for me, you are mine forever.

You seem to be suggesting that the new generation of warrior would fire upon the citizens of USA.

Oh, they are programmed to fire upon anybody on orders.

"Warrior," I say? Understand that a primary function of orthocratic war is to engage the warrior spirit in man (in the event that any such spirit has survived the educational process) and to channel that energy into military rigors. Otherwise that spirit could become a hazard to the orthocracy.

In Iraq, a lean-mean professional army gets combat-hardened through consecutive tours of duty. This management technique produces a core of reliably programmed personnel, while the weaker fall away into psychosis and suicide.

The US president just announced that all troops will be out of Iraq by Christmas, 2011.

The 13 Rules: 1. Keep them weak. **2.** Keep them dumb, **3.** Keep them scared. **4.** Control all their resources. **5.** Divide and conquer. **6.** Control their rhythm and pace. **7.** Control their chemistry. **8.** Control their sex. **9.** Jack them around. **10.** Use coercion routinely, brute force when necessary. **11.** Use deception routinely, the Big Lie when necessary. **12.** None of this can show. **13.** This is The System, there shall be no other.

Meanwhile, over time, and by one scenario or another, a fatigued and battered Iraq will ultimately surrender its territory to the greater orthocratic good.

It is important for good orthocrats to think positively.

5. The Economic Collapse

Experts say, "The capitalist system is breaking down." What do you say, Orthocracy, is the system breaking down?

I am the system, I am not "capitalism," and I am not breaking down. I am operating as designed. A well organized orthocratic economy can be expanded or contracted as deemed expedient for purposes of social management, which is the real bottom line. You get the boom and the inevitable bust. Then my media call upon their stable of academic economists, who reliably contrive a plausible long-winded narrative ("mistakes" were made, some "bad apples" committed this or that crime). Meanwhile, boom-and-bust remains the cyclical orthocratic norm.

Boom-and-bust is the Darwinian Rule-9 of orthocratic economics. Each jack-around shakes out the weak, thus empowering the old established orthocrats. Orthocracy insists that society at large be managed as a corporation. A corporation can

---

The 13 Rules: 1. Keep them weak. **2.** Keep them dumb, **3.** Keep them scared. **4.** Control all their resources. **5.** Divide and conquer. **6.** Control their rhythm and pace. **7.** Control their chemistry. **8.** Control their sex. **9.** Jack them around. **10.** Use coercion routinely, brute force when necessary. **11.** Use deception routinely, the Big Lie when necessary. **12.** None of this can show. **13.** This is The System, there shall be no other.

merge with another, can rename and rebrand itself, reduce its population, and it can even dissolve and disappear if it wants to.

Desirable are financial orthocracies that can leverage manipulations of entire economies. Desirable are huge conglomerated industrial orthocracies that can lay off a hundred thousand while retaining essential function.

A corporation fires people, sure, Orthocracy, but I ask – with some trepidation – in society at large, what would be the equivalent of the lay-off?

You would have to call it *genocide*, I suppose. The corporate reorganization is often about eliminating a category of personnel called "dead wood."

But the issue here is called Economic Collapse, and it is a different animal from the routine boom-and-bust oscillation. The current crisis is a phase of a corporate reorganization that will enable The Great Step Forward, if I may sloganize. Corporate reorganization is about the elimination of old, obsolete structures and systems, and other "dead wood."

Obsolete people, that is.

The 13 Rules: 1. Keep them weak. **2.** Keep them dumb. **3.** Keep them scared. **4.** Control all their resources. **5.** Divide and conquer. **6.** Control their rhythm and pace. **7.** Control their chemistry. **8.** Control their sex. **9.** Jack them around. **10.** Use coercion routinely, brute force when necessary. **11.** Use deception routinely, the Big Lie when necessary. **12.** None of this can show. **13.** This is The System, there shall be no other.

Them, too. Now a corporation can reorganize by executive order, but the larger orthocracy is not yet so empowered. It must become so. This project will require Rule-10 recourse, a war. Depressions are generally followed by wars, the economic hardships being a softening up, so to speak, of the targeted population (Rule 1).

Next issue.

6. Privacy

People complain their privacy is being invaded by government agencies and corporations. The National Security Agency is constructing a gigantic facility in Utah to soak up and analyze all internet and telephone communications. Airport security routinely x-rays travelers and pats down their bodies. Facebook has been exposed as a surveillance tool. Video cameras are everywhere.

I know everything (Rule 4). You know nothing (Rule 2).

But, Orthocracy, why must you know everything?

Because effective management depends upon the managed being thoroughly known in behavior and character profile.

The 13 Rules: 1. Keep them weak. **2.** Keep them dumb, **3.** Keep them scared. **4.** Control all their resources. **5.** Divide and conquer. **6.** Control their rhythm and pace. **7.** Control their chemistry. **8.** Control their sex. **9.** Jack them around. **10.** Use coercion routinely, brute force when necessary. **11.** Use deception routinely, the Big Lie when necessary. **12.** None of this can show. **13.** This is The System, there shall be no other.

Hmm,"effective management". Indeed you have said that humanity is a management problem.

Today there is some whining because the surveillance standards everyone has become accustomed to in the workplace are finally being applied to society at large. Why should there be a difference? Get used to it.

But humanity insists that privacy is a God-given right.

Let me parse that stupid sentence, Editor George: 1. Show me the rule that applies. 2. Who's this God who grants this alleged right anyway? 3. You say humanity "insists" on privacy, but my urine-testing program went down like white bread, in the workplace, then in the army, the prisons, the schools and sports. With this very intimate inspection: No problem. You say that humanity "insists." What kind of insistence is that? Next: home-testing via the new code-mandated analytical family toilet, with a data-link to the smart grid.

By the way, George, have you been tested lately?

The 13 Rules: 1. Keep them weak. **2.** Keep them dumb. **3.** Keep them scared. **4.** Control all their resources. **5.** Divide and conquer. **6.** Control their rhythm and pace. **7.** Control their chemistry. **8.** Control their sex. **9.** Jack them around. **10.** Use coercion routinely, brute force when necessary. **11.** Use deception routinely, the Big Lie when necessary. **12.** None of this can show. **13.** This is The System, there shall be no other.

7. Energy

Industrial society seems to be engaged in an endless struggle to find the energy necessary to drive its wheels. But how can this be accomplished without environmental destruction?

Everybody knows that energy is scarce. Everybody knows that the extraction of energy resources is an arduous and hazardous process. Everybody knows that energy resources are nearing exhaustion and that energy is an increasingly expensive commodity. Everybody knows that the consumption of any energy resource inevitably creates pollution.

Why does everybody know this? Because I tell them so. Energy-scarcity is an established orthocratic truth. So please turn out the lights.

Are you suggesting that energy-scarcity is just another of your myths? Is it Orthocracy the myth-maker here again?

Indeed, I *am* the myth-maker, and the myth of energy scarcity is a fundamental official truth of orthocratic science, as it is a pillar of orthocratic economics.

But science is presumed to be detached, disinterested, objective, transcendent. It is not supposed to be myth.

Disinterested is the desired image (Rule 11), but my science is really about orthocratic expediency.

The 13 Rules: 1. Keep them weak. **2.** Keep them dumb, **3.** Keep them scared. **4.** Control all their resources. **5.** Divide and conquer. **6.** Control their rhythm and pace. **7.** Control their chemistry. **8.** Control their sex. **9.** Jack them around. **10.** Use coercion routinely, brute force when necessary. **11.** Use deception routinely, the Big Lie when necessary. **12.** None of this can show. **13.** This is The System, there shall be no other.

Please understand that science is too important to be left to the vagaries of unfettered inquiry. Good scientists understand this principle.

But the scarcity of energy is an established scientific consensus.

My science is a consensus science. Appreciate my clout. I am able to engineer any scientific or scholarly consensus expedient to my ends by the selective dispensation of financial grants and academic chairs.

Your mythology says pollution is inevitable when energy is consumed. So what about this new crisis from CO2? What about this global-warming theory?

For my weather mod, that theory is a great cover (Rule 12).

Of course, the addition of a chemical to the atmosphere has never had the slightest effect on the weather and never will. Weather is not chemistry. Weather is a phenomenon of energies, electrical and more exotic. However, if I've got you thinking chemistry (Rule 2), then the true science of weather has been reserved for me and my manipulations (Rule 4).

The theory does seem to attribute drought and violent storms to the dreaded green-house gases. But you are saying

---

The 13 Rules: 1. Keep them weak. **2.** Keep them dumb. **3.** Keep them scared. **4.** Control all their resources. **5.** Divide and conquer. **6.** Control their rhythm and pace. **7.** Control their chemistry. **8.** Control their sex. **9.** Jack them around. **10.** Use coercion routinely, brute force when necessary. **11.** Use deception routinely, the Big Lie when necessary. **12.** None of this can show. **13.** This is The System, there shall be no other.

these disasters are your work? Amazing that you admit to weather-modification.

Weather is too important to geopolitics to be left to the vagaries of nature. Weather must be rigorously managed like everything else.

Managed for what results in particular?

The hurricane, for example, is a useful tool for clearing old real estate in order to develop the new, and it is deniable, whereas bombing is not. For example, a lot of coastal real estate is wasted on mediocre structures that will be be replaced by high-rise ocean-view condos. In respect to drought: if rainfall can be managed, then the distribution of population can be managed.

Global-warming's most prominent politician recently declared that the "denialist" has become as unpopular as the "racist" — a very unflattering appellation in liberal circles.

That politician is a great orthocrat.

I mean the campus doubter cannot get a date.

The 13 Rules: 1. Keep them weak. **2.** Keep them dumb, **3.** Keep them scared. **4.** Control all their resources. **5.** Divide and conquer. **6.** Control their rhythm and pace. **7.** Control their chemistry. **8.** Control their sex. **9.** Jack them around. **10.** Use coercion routinely, brute force when necessary. **11.** Use deception routinely, the Big Lie when necessary. **12.** None of this can show. **13.** This is The System, there shall be no other.

This fashionable global-warming climate-change theory has another orthocratic utility shrouded under Rule 12, and that is the ordering of industry, its growth and nongrowth, by means of a global system of offsets and credits.

Industrial development cannot take care of itself?

Of course not. Energy cannot be distributed Willy-nilly. The industries of the planet cannot be left to the vagaries of spontaneous growth. Rule 1 demands the maintenance of a balance of powerlessness among orthocratic states. So global-warming is about offsets and credits.

Meanwhile, as we finally move on, George, be sure to mind your carbon imprint. I refer to the carbon emissions from your driving, heating, cooking, and the other gross energy consumptions of your careless lifestyle.

It is necessary also to factor in your exhalations, eructations, and flatuations, as well as the eructations and flatuations of all the animals you consume. It goes on and on, environmental offenses too numerous to mention. You and all of your gaseous fellow humans must take responsibility for your respective carbon footprints. Habits must change. Society must change, globally. This is the major challenge to humanity today, don't you know.

The 13 Rules: 1. Keep them weak. **2.** Keep them dumb. **3.** Keep them scared. **4.** Control all their resources. **5.** Divide and conquer. **6.** Control their rhythm and pace. **7.** Control their chemistry. **8.** Control their sex. **9.** Jack them around. **10.** Use coercion routinely, brute force when necessary. **11.** Use deception routinely, the Big Lie when necessary. **12.** None of this can show. **13.** This is The System, there shall be no other.

88 | Orthocracy Speaks

As we speak, certain stringent standards and metrics are being defined by the emerging orthocracy of sustainability. You want to be within the established carbon-imprint specifications, George, in order to qualify for the new green era, lest you be marked as unsustainable.

That is an ominous threat, Orthocracy. I would not want to speculate on the fate of those who are marked as "unsustainable."

The sustainable planet of the future will be reduced to about 500 million clean, cheerful, well-behaved orthocrats. You want to be among them, George. So mind your carbon imprint.

This global-warming may be fashionable today, but readers of this in the future may have no idea what we are talking about. When global-warming's orthocratic mission is accomplished, the issue will go down the memory tube along with some other fashions of scientific theory. Remember the ozone hole?

Vaguely. But, Orthocracy, all of science cannot function on your mythic orthocratic constructs. An honest science must be practiced somewhere or no technology would work.

True. You could say that there are three levels of science. Level-1 is the science of an upper orthocracy

---

The 13 Rules: 1. Keep them weak. **2.** Keep them dumb, **3.** Keep them scared. **4.** Control all their resources. **5.** Divide and conquer. **6.** Control their rhythm and pace. **7.** Control their chemistry. **8.** Control their sex. **9.** Jack them around. **10.** Use coercion routinely, brute force when necessary. **11.** Use deception routinely, the Big Lie when necessary. **12.** None of this can show. **13.** This is The System, there shall be no other.

that conducts a more permissive research, but its activity is secret, being governed by Rule 12. Level-1 research is compartmentalized so that no researcher can see the whole. Level 1 research is accessible only to the investigated and cleared.

The science that most people know is at Level 2, an orthocratic science for public consumption. It has been called "official science." There is also a Level 3, a permissive science conducted by inventors and experimenters in basements and garages. Orthocratic science has the job of policing this element.

So you are saying that science must be policed?

Orthocratic science must set the limits of technological possibility and enforce those limits.

Limits? Hmmmm. What about Nicola Tesla's later inventions? And what happened to cold fusion, anyway?

The technologies you speak of are disruptive technologies.

Disruptive of what?

The 13 Rules: 1. Keep them weak. **2.** Keep them dumb, **3.** Keep them scared. **4.** Control all their resources. **5.** Divide and conquer. **6.** Control their rhythm and pace. **7.** Control their chemistry. **8.** Control their sex. **9.** Jack them around. **10.** Use coercion routinely, brute force when necessary. **11.** Use deception routinely, the Big Lie when necessary. **12.** None of this can show. **13.** This is The System, there shall be no other.

Disruptive of me and my model of social functioning. Free energy is a great threat to Rules 1 and 4 and maybe some others.

Now you are asking a lot of questions, Editor George, and you are dragging this entry out. I feel we are getting near the end of this entire opus, and I'm getting eager to wrap it up. Orthocracy has spoken enough.

OK, but science is important to me.

Apparently, but you should not get hung up on the integrity of it. Nobody else does.

8. Mountain-top Removal

I guess such extreme excavation is an expeditious way to extract coal, Orthocracy, but the practice is more unpopular than the clear-cutting of forests, I mean from the environmental point of view.

From the view of the tree-hugging nature-sentimentalist, you mean, but of course that's not my point of view. Appreciate, however, that I do have my own orthocratic environmentalism. Mountain-top removal, and clear-cutting as well, are perfectly consistent with it.

The 13 Rules: 1. Keep them weak. **2.** Keep them dumb, **3.** Keep them scared. **4.** Control all their resources. **5.** Divide and conquer. **6.** Control their rhythm and pace. **7.** Control their chemistry. **8.** Control their sex. **9.** Jack them around. **10.** Use coercion routinely, brute force when necessary. **11.** Use deception routinely, the Big Lie when necessary. **12.** None of this can show. **13.** This is The System, there shall be no other.

"An orthocratic environmentalism?" Is that not an oxymoron?

In the lexicon of the tree-huggers perhaps, but in my tongue...

That would be orthocratese, correct?

I suppose, Editor George, but the point is that I am the true environmentalist. In respect to the mountain-top removal and the clear-cutting, please understand that certain outcomes favorable to orthocratic environmentalism may trump all the benefits of cheap and easy extraction. In truth, the extracted coal and its dollar profits soon go up in smoke, but the excavation lasts forever.

Orthocracy, forgive my stupidity. I'm afraid the logic here escapes me. What conceivably could be the benefits derived from mowing down ancient forests and leveling the very mountains they stand upon.

Think: When the rebel bands retreat, where do they go?

Hmm, into the hills?

The 13 Rules: 1. Keep them weak. **2.** Keep them dumb. **3.** Keep them scared. **4.** Control all their resources. **5.** Divide and conquer. **6.** Control their rhythm and pace. **7.** Control their chemistry. **8.** Control their sex. **9.** Jack them around. **10.** Use coercion routinely, brute force when necessary. **11.** Use deception routinely, the Big Lie when necessary. **12.** None of this can show. **13.** This is The System, there shall be no other.

Yes, into the forested mountains. If such is available. Are you beginning to see at least the military benefits of these bold excavations?

No place to hide?

Exactly. Now consider how those forested mountains might also provide our putative rebels with foraged food, game, firewood, and fish from free-running streams. But beyond the military advantage, consider how such sylvan amenities might also encourage homesteaders, campers, and other squatters to carve out of the wilderness atavistic lifestyles remote from urban orthocratic institutions.

Clear-cutting and mountain-top removal can decisively excavate these amenities out of existence. Effective also are certain aerial spraying programs as well as forest-management styles encouraging of eventual conflagration.

Next issue.

9. The Gulf Oil Spill

In the news, fishermen complain that the Gulf is dying as a food source, and residents are voicing health complaints. Environmentalists are up in arms.

The 13 Rules: 1. Keep them weak. **2.** Keep them dumb, **3.** Keep them scared. **4.** Control all their resources. **5.** Divide and conquer. **6.** Control their rhythm and pace. **7.** Control their chemistry. **8.** Control their sex. **9.** Jack them around. **10.** Use coercion routinely, brute force when necessary. **11.** Use deception routinely, the Big Lie when necessary. **12.** None of this can show. **13.** This is The System, there shall be no other.

There is bound to be some whining over an incident like this. Anyway, my creative scientists have invented an oil-devouring bacterium. So everything will be OK in time.

In respect to the food-source issue, please understand a fundamental here. The well organized orthocracy scrupulously maintains the power to starve its population at will. Consequently, food cannot be easily extractable by just anyone – not from the forests and not from the oceans, rivers, lakes, or streams. Colonies of fishermen hanging out and supporting themselves from prolific waters: that is in defiance of Rule 4. The proper source for food is the supermarket, which is supplied on a just-in-time basis by centralized food processors.

As to those health complaints, I refer you to Rule 1. Also at work here is Rule 7.

Are you saying, Orthocracy, that this environmental disaster was created deliberately?

This particular disaster specifically precipitated by direct intentional action? Not necessarily. Outcomes consistent with the rules of rule can occur by default. It a matter of setting up the conditions.

There were thousands of oil platforms operating in the Gulf. This being allowed, and Murphy's Law being continuously in effect, wouldn't disaster be inevitable

---

The 13 Rules: 1. Keep them weak. **2.** Keep them dumb. **3.** Keep them scared. **4.** Control all their resources. **5.** Divide and conquer. **6.** Control their rhythm and pace. **7.** Control their chemistry. **8.** Control their sex. **9.** Jack them around. **10.** Use coercion routinely, brute force when necessary. **11.** Use deception routinely, the Big Lie when necessary. **12.** None of this can show. **13.** This is The System, there shall be no other.

under these conditions, especially if new drilling depths and pressures were ventured? So why is this permitted?

The oil platforms you refer to are licensed by planning procedures, which are orthocratic processes responsibly conducted by orthocratic institutions (oil corporations and their government regulators in this case) operating under the usual orthocratic rules.

Now, about your citation of Murphy's Law and the inevitability of disaster under these conditions: This would seem to be a plausible and persuasive argument. However it is an argument that would never be considered by the orthocrats empowered to allow or disallow the project.

For example, in the public permitting process, the environmentalist-intervenor may draw grim scenarios of leaks, blow-outs, and explosions and the resulting pollution and its negative impacts on ocean sustainability and human health. He will support his scenarios with convincing data painstakingly assembled. These undesirable environmental outcomes are inevitable under the circumstances, he will argue, which may be correct.

In arguing his case, the intervenor may sense a particular impatience and anger in the presiding orthocrats, as if public intervention in itself were somehow improper and unwelcome, which it is. Appreciate that the applicable rules (1, 4, and 7) are expressed in imperative sentences that designate

---

The 13 Rules: 1. Keep them weak. **2.** Keep them dumb, **3.** Keep them scared. **4.** Control all their resources. **5.** Divide and conquer. **6.** Control their rhythm and pace. **7.** Control their chemistry. **8.** Control their sex. **9.** Jack them around. **10.** Use coercion routinely, brute force when necessary. **11.** Use deception routinely, the Big Lie when necessary. **12.** None of this can show. **13.** This is The System, there shall be no other.

the orthocracy as the sole actor in these matters – regardless of what any annoying environmental laws may say about public access.

When, finally, the intervenor's arguments get completely ignored and the case is decided against him, he will express dismay and righteous indignation: "It's the greed!" he will cry. "It's the money!"

The money? The greed? Not necessarily. Lurking in the background, acknowledged by no one but ultimately prevailing by default, are my ineluctable, ineffable, transcendent rules of rule.

The above is a glimpse into the bureaucratics by which the orthocracy designs your world. Outraged citizens think that they can appeal their environmental issues to orthocratic authority. Do you see why this is absurd?

10. Barack Hussein Obama

This president has caused great wonderment. What says Orthocracy about this phenomenon?

He is a great orthocrat. Very plausible, very, very smooth.

Orthocracy, you didn't happen to spend your college years at ... never mind.

The 13 Rules: 1. Keep them weak. **2.** Keep them dumb. **3.** Keep them scared. **4.** Control all their resources. **5.** Divide and conquer. **6.** Control their rhythm and pace. **7.** Control their chemistry. **8.** Control their sex. **9.** Jack them around. **10.** Use coercion routinely, brute force when necessary. **11.** Use deception routinely, the Big Lie when necessary. **12.** None of this can show. **13.** This is The System, there shall be no other.

What? Anyway, Editor George, your chosen issue here: Is it not a departure from our editorial commitment to discuss only the What of my system, not the Who of it?

But is Obama one of the ultimate Who's, really?

That is a most perceptive question, Editor George. Actually, no, he is just the premier employee of the real who's, and a temporary one at that. A great fog of hyperbole surrounds "the leader of the free world," That fog gets particularly dense at election time, conveniently obscuring all other news (Rule 12).

In truth the exalted President is just an interim public-relations man for the orthocracy, and Obama is a very smooth one. He is exceptionally proficient at the prevarication skills demanded by Rule 11. The president also serves as a lightning rod for strikes which otherwise might hit me.

So the president is a symbol, another of your orthocratic constructs?

In the future the president will be a hologram.

I think Obama also qualifies for discussion because he is iconic. He also qualifies for this particular chapter as an issue in himself. He is a black man in a white nation.

The 13 Rules: 1. Keep them weak. **2.** Keep them dumb, **3.** Keep them scared. **4.** Control all their resources. **5.** Divide and conquer. **6.** Control their rhythm and pace. **7.** Control their chemistry. **8.** Control their sex. **9.** Jack them around. **10.** Use coercion routinely, brute force when necessary. **11.** Use deception routinely, the Big Lie when necessary. **12.** None of this can show. **13.** This is The System, there shall be no other.

He is believed by many to be of foreign birth. These issues hover over the Obama presidency.

Perceptive again George. You have identified two of Obama's greatest assets as a candidate. Some may wonder how this junior senator was suddenly catapulted above others into the status of serious presidential contender.

It does seem that, in any election, a particular candidate suddenly gets anointed, and then all the attention goes to him. But how could Obama's citizenship and race be anything but liabilities? Orthocratically, I guess Rule 5 would benefit from the racism.

Indeed, Rule 5 is what race is all about.

Rule 5: racist against liberal. Also I can see how the citizenship issue would pit the patriotic types against the honor-diversity types.

True, Also appreciate Obama as a Rule-9 phenomenon. The racists and the patriots wake up one November morning to a black president whose papers are not quite in order. What a marvelous jack-around.

Insulting.

The 13 Rules: 1. Keep them weak. **2.** Keep them dumb. **3.** Keep them scared. **4.** Control all their resources. **5.** Divide and conquer. **6.** Control their rhythm and pace. **7.** Control their chemistry. **8.** Control their sex. **9.** Jack them around. **10.** Use coercion routinely, brute force when necessary. **11.** Use deception routinely, the Big Lie when necessary. **12.** None of this can show. **13.** This is The System, there shall be no other.

True. A measure of insult in the presidential choice has become a tradition. But in particular, one needs to appreciate the ambiguity here and its great utility. Writers know the uses of ambiguity, George. I have my own uses. Neither Obama's citizenship nor his race is clear-cut. One parent is white, the other black. Perfect ambiguity. Was he born in Hawaii or in Kenya? Is he American or African? Go figure.

The media gives this challenge to presidential legitimacy no official status, but it does grant just enough right-wing airtime to keep these issues burning beneath the surface in the national subconscious.

Just where you like to work. But what is the value to you of this particular ambiguity?

It is excellent conditioning for a nation that will ultimately have to submit to governance by a centralized orthocratic authority headquartered in Brussels or Hong Kong. Obama is the perfect transitional president.

Speaking of ambiguity, there is also the matter of the president's name and its equation, but for a single letter, with Osama. Even veteran broadcasters make the inevitable Freudian slip, confusing the designated leader with the designated enemy. Also consider the "Hussein" equation.

The 13 Rules: 1. Keep them weak. **2.** Keep them dumb, **3.** Keep them scared. **4.** Control all their resources. **5.** Divide and conquer. **6.** Control their rhythm and pace. **7.** Control their chemistry. **8.** Control their sex. **9.** Jack them around. **10.** Use coercion routinely, brute force when necessary. **11.** Use deception routinely, the Big Lie when necessary. **12.** None of this can show. **13.** This is The System, there shall be no other.

Rule 9, Editor George. A lovely piece of orthocratic poetry is Barack Hussein Obama.

11. Immigration

The issue burns especially in USA and Europe. An alien third-world demographic suddenly materializes in a first-world city, disturbing the established neighborhood society, especially when it realizes that the aliens are government subsidized.

Immigration is a Rule-5 phenomenon. Various populations around the globe get displaced from certain territories. Often these are territories targeted for orthocratic development under the Rule-13 imperative.

Fragments of the targeted populations who manage to survive the famine, the bombing, the spraying, or whatever the displacement strategy, become migratory and helpless (Rule 1). To some these people are a nuisance, but to others they become a resource – yes, Mr. Marxist, a cheap labor resource – but this expendable population also becomes a resource for social engineering, always the bottom line.

By the introduction of alien groups, cities can be partitioned by invisible walls of resentment and fear. Established neighborhoods and cultures can be dispersed and replaced. Thus coherent demographics,

---

The 13 Rules: 1. Keep them weak. **2.** Keep them dumb. **3.** Keep them scared. **4.** Control all their resources. **5.** Divide and conquer. **6.** Control their rhythm and pace. **7.** Control their chemistry. **8.** Control their sex. **9.** Jack them around. **10.** Use coercion routinely, brute force when necessary. **11.** Use deception routinely, the Big Lie when necessary. **12.** None of this can show. **13.** This is The System, there shall be no other.

always threatening to my rule, can be successfully fragmented in accordance with Rule 5.

As a Rule-5 dividend comes conflict on the political stage between the anti-immigration people and the honor-diversity folks, and this controversy played very loudly obscures, in accordance with Rule 12, the social engineering action of Rule 5 and the system.

Next issue.

12. Chemtrails, Black Helicopters, UFO's, Men in Black

These issues are barely discussable in polite society, but I suspect they might be orthocratic phenomena. Can you throw some light on these mysteries?

What chemtrails? What black helicopters? What UFO's? What men in black? All good orthocrats know that none of these exist (Rule 12).

On the other hand ...

I see, Orthocracy. Some more of your ambiguity.

Editor George, chapter by chapter, you become smarter and smarter. Yes, ambiguity, ambivalence, psychic inner-conflict and division, including social division between the believers and the nonbelievers.

The 13 Rules: 1. Keep them weak. **2.** Keep them dumb, **3.** Keep them scared. **4.** Control all their resources. **5.** Divide and conquer. **6.** Control their rhythm and pace. **7.** Control their chemistry. **8.** Control their sex. **9.** Jack them around. **10.** Use coercion routinely, brute force when necessary. **11.** Use deception routinely, the Big Lie when necessary. **12.** None of this can show. **13.** This is The System, there shall be no other.

Rule 5 is at work here, but Rule 3 benefits as well, and Rule 9 gets some exercise, too.

But these phenomena really do exist in the shadows. I myself witnessed a swarm of black helicopters perform a two-hour combat exercise over downtown. Soldiers in black were seen hanging out the doors holding automatic rifles. This episode was so conspicuous and undeniable that the local daily had to print the taboo term "black helicopter." So the incident had official recognition.

But now when you mention the incident to friends?

They get a bit embarrassed.

On to the next issue then. Just one more issue to go. Let's get this book done. I have lots of work to do. I have spoken enough on my system for any reader to appreciate its elegance, beauty, and spiritual purity.

Gee, orthocracy, next you will be boasting that your system is humanitarian.

I leave that to my politicians.

The 13 Rules: 1. Keep them weak. **2.** Keep them dumb. **3.** Keep them scared. **4.** Control all their resources. **5.** Divide and conquer. **6.** Control their rhythm and pace. **7.** Control their chemistry. **8.** Control their sex. **9.** Jack them around. **10.** Use coercion routinely, brute force when necessary. **11.** Use deception routinely, the Big Lie when necessary. **12.** None of this can show. **13.** This is The System, there shall be no other.

13. Drone Attacks

In the news: A US citizen, a designated terrorist, is targeted for assassination in Yemen by presidential order. A drone fires two Hellfire missiles into his car, killing him and a companion. In Washington, demonstrators are repelled by pepper spray as they try to break into the Smithsonian Space museum to protest a drone exhibit. This is becoming a hot issue. What says Orthocracy?

It is unfortunate that this has become a hot issue, for the drone promises great Rule-12 advantages. "Drone" is an archaic term for this advanced aerial-robotic weapon, isn't it? But my Rule 12 likes euphemisms. Editor George, please understand that a properly organized orthocracy should have the power to neutralize any troublemaker or potential troublemaker at any time by executive order or less and to employ state-of-the-art technology in doing so.

You invoke Rule 12, Orthocracy, but this attack in Yemen was not covert. it was announced triumphantly by the US president himself. Wasn't this unusually brazen? In fact, Orthocracy, your behavior seems abnormally up-front in many departments these days, as if you were even relaxing Rule 12 a bit.

An astute observation, Editor George. About that Yemen drone attack: I don't know what all the fuss

---

The 13 Rules: 1. Keep them weak. **2.** Keep them dumb, **3.** Keep them scared. **4.** Control all their resources. **5.** Divide and conquer. **6.** Control their rhythm and pace. **7.** Control their chemistry. **8.** Control their sex. **9.** Jack them around. **10.** Use coercion routinely, brute force when necessary. **11.** Use deception routinely, the Big Lie when necessary. **12.** None of this can show. **13.** This is The System, there shall be no other.

is. The foundation was laid for such executions with the Bin-Laden "hit." The story went down. No one objected, thus certifying the next progressive step, which is the aerial-robotic hit, and why should a US citizen be exempt?

Your observation about a new audacity is correct, though, George, I do have a new self-confidence. Orthocracy has been on a roll in recent years. I am enjoying some great advances in orthocratic power. Foundations have been laid, and now is the time to move on to The New-World Order, The Global Orthocratic Superstate, The Carbon-free Green Planetary Nation, or whatever slogan is ultimately adopted. The new constitution and the sloganeering are under draft at various international meetings. While orthocracy takes The Great Step Forward, the world must accustom itself to a new audacity of orthocratic action.

Like throwing missiles at the designated enemy and then bragging about it on TV.

Yes, Rule 12 recedes a bit, and a little more is shown of the terrible me.

By "great advances in orthocratic power" do you mean advances in warfare technology, like the drones?

The 13 Rules: 1. Keep them weak. **2.** Keep them dumb. **3.** Keep them scared. **4.** Control all their resources. **5.** Divide and conquer. **6.** Control their rhythm and pace. **7.** Control their chemistry. **8.** Control their sex. **9.** Jack them around. **10.** Use coercion routinely, brute force when necessary. **11.** Use deception routinely, the Big Lie when necessary. **12.** None of this can show. **13.** This is The System, there shall be no other.

Not necessarily. The greatest advances have been made in the domains of Rules 11 and 12, the domains of mind-management. For example, in respect to unilateral assassination, by drone or whatever, you will notice that the threshold of acceptability has just been moved forward.

Yes, I am the true progressive.

But, back to the technology, what does the future hold, I ask with some trepidation?

The automation of warfare does take a leap forward with the drone technology, but, in the near future, assassination by robotic aircraft will seem but a crude tool. Consider the new satellite technology, called Skypurge, already in prototype.

Skypurge?

Skypurge is a satellite-platform high-energy electric-ray weapon (SHEW). I am reading from the tech manual, already in draft. A Skypurge hit is carried out as follows: The target's GPS location (determined by cell-phone access, optical satellite, or ground observer) is communicated to Skypurge satellite's computer, which, in turn, focuses upon said target the high-energy UV laser (HUV), this

---

The 13 Rules: 1. Keep them weak. **2.** Keep them dumb, **3.** Keep them scared. **4.** Control all their resources. **5.** Divide and conquer. **6.** Control their rhythm and pace. **7.** Control their chemistry. **8.** Control their sex. **9.** Jack them around. **10.** Use coercion routinely, brute force when necessary. **11.** Use deception routinely, the Big Lie when necessary. **12.** None of this can show. **13.** This is The System, there shall be no other.

ray creating an ionized conductive medium that can carry an instantaneous 2-million-joule capacitive electric discharge, which energizes said target with 1200 amperes at 200,000 volts head-to-toe, causing instantaneous vaporization. Unlike robotic aircraft, there will be no human controller in some remote bunker selecting the target. It is all computerized. The list of candidates is scanned and by some algorithm a decision made, which the Skypurge computer executes.

Skypurge has potential as a straffing weapon, I would imagine.

Oh, sure. It can vaporize a tribal village in a fraction of the time of drone attacks.

Like throwing lightning bolts. God-like. The power of Thor.

Godlike I intend to be. My power of Thor is just one more reason why everybody should behave like good orthocrats and give me no problems.

The 13 Rules: 1. Keep them weak. **2.** Keep them dumb. **3.** Keep them scared. **4.** Control all their resources. **5.** Divide and conquer. **6.** Control their rhythm and pace. **7.** Control their chemistry. **8.** Control their sex. **9.** Jack them around. **10.** Use coercion routinely, brute force when necessary. **11.** Use deception routinely, the Big Lie when necessary. **12.** None of this can show. **13.** This is The System, there shall be no other.

Also by George Trinkaus:

in print:
Tesla Technology
Lost Inventions, Radio Tesla,
Tesla Coil, Son of Tesla Coil
now in a combined edition

High Voltage Press

online:
Magnetic Amplifiers, NBC Spins 911, Nerd Flu,
Tesla Mystique, Tesla Electrotherapy,
How the Chronicle *Invented AIDS*

teslapress.com

Made in the USA
San Bernardino, CA
16 September 2016